Playwriting across the curriculum

This book is a guide to introducing ⬛⬛⬛⬛⬛⬛⬛⬛⬛ the secondary English curriculum at key s⬛⬛⬛ ...ง แเ TEEP (Teacher Effectiveness Enhancement Programme) framework. The authors also provide a particular focus on applying this versatile scheme of work to other areas of the curriculum, including Citizenship and PSHE.

Playwriting Across the Curriculum also contains schemes of work for:

- pupils with special educational needs (SEN)
- pupils with English as an additional language (EAL)
- adaptation to Adult Literacy Core Curriculum.

Its coverage of specific plays as part of the scheme ensures that students will engage with contemporary writing in their learning. This is an essential resource for anyone wanting to teach playwriting at secondary school level.

Caroline Jester is Dramaturg at Birmingham Repertory Theatre, and led Transmissions, the company's award winning young writers' programme, for ten years. She also works as a director, has taught on the MPhil in Playwriting at Birmingham University and develops digital and international playwriting programmes.

Claire Stoneman is Assistant Headteacher at Dame Elizabeth Cadbury Technology College, Bournville, Birmingham, where she leads teaching and learning, teachers' continuing professional development, and school-based action research in partnership with Birmingham City University. She has collaborated with the Birmingham Repertory Theatre for a number of years. Claire is also a TEEP trainer and a doctoral researcher at the University of Birmingham.

Playwriting Across the Curriculum

Caroline Jester and Claire Stoneman

Routledge
Taylor & Francis Group

LONDON AND NEW YORK

First published 2012
by Routledge
2 Park Square, Milton Park, Abingdon, Oxon OX14 4RN

Simultaneously published in the USA and Canada
by Routledge
711 Third Avenue, New York, NY 10017

Routledge is an imprint of the Taylor & Francis Group, an informa business

British Library Cataloguing in Publication Data
A catalogue record for this book is available from the British Library

Library of Congress Cataloging in Publication Data
Jester, Caroline.
Playwriting across the curriculum / Caroline Jester and Claire Stoneman.
p. cm.
Includes bibliographical references.
1. Playwriting--Study and teaching. I. Stoneman, Claire. II. Title.
PN1661.J47 2011
808.2071--dc22
2011014886

ISBN: 978-0-415-59095-2 (hbk)
ISBN: 978-0-415-59096-9 (pbk)
ISBN: 978-0-203-81620-2 (ebk)

Typeset in Helvetica
by Saxon Graphics Ltd, Derby

MIX
Paper from
responsible sources
FSC
www.fsc.org   FSC® C004839

Printed and bound in Great Britain by the MPG Books Group

Contents

For downloadable PDF versions of lesson plans and additional resources, please visit www.routledge.com/9780415590969

Acknowledgements

The material in this book has been developed over a number of years and would not have been possible without the sharing and exchange of ideas. As ideas move from one formation into another it is often difficult to remember where they came from, but this book owes a lot to the inspirational playwriting workshops led by Noël Greig and Carl Miller for the Birmingham Repertory Theatre's Young Writers' Programme, 'Transmissions', between 1999 and 2008. We would also like to thank Joshua Dalledonne, Fiona King and Clare Lovell for trying out these ideas and for their feedback. We're grateful for the continued support and recognition of its value and we would like to thank Dee Palmer-Jones, Arlene Crewdson and everyone who has helped us to experiment along the way.

All the schools involved over the years have been very supportive, but a particular thank you must go to the following schools for trialling these schemes of work, for their feedback in shaping the work and for sharing our enthusiasm for the aims of this book: Calthorpe School, Birmingham; St Alban's Academy, Birmingham; Shenley Academy, Birmingham; Harborne Academy, Birmingham; Yardleys School, Birmingham; Batmans Hill PRU, Tipton; George Dixon International School, Birmingham; Pittville School, Cheltenham. Thanks especially to all the amazing students.

An extra special thank you must go to Noël Greig for his teaching along the way and support of this book in its early stages.

The author and publishers would like to thank the copyright holders for permission to reproduce extracts from the following:

Extract from *The Mother Ship* by Douglas Maxwell. Included by kind permission of Oberon Books Ltd, 521 Caledonian Road, London N7 9RH. info@Oberonbooks.com.

viii   Acknowledgements

Extract from *Stolen Secrets* by Fin Kennedy. Included by kind permission of Nick Hern Books Ltd from the publication *Urban Girl's Guide to Camping and other plays* published by Nick Hern Books Ltd, 2010.

Extract from *Urban Girl's Guide to Camping* by Fin Kennedy. Included by kind permission of Nick Hern Books Ltd from the publication *Urban Girl's Guide to Camping and other plays* published by Nick Hern Books Ltd, 2010.

Extract from *Baby Girl* © Roy Williams 2007, from the publication *NT Connections 2007: New Plays for Young People* published by Faber and Faber Ltd, 2007.

Extract from *The Miracle* by Lin Coghlan. Included by kind permission of United Agents Ltd on behalf of Lin Coghlan from the publication *Shell Connections 2006: New Plays for Young People* published by Faber and Faber Ltd, 2007.

Extract from *School Journey to the Centre of the Earth* by Daisy Campbell, with Ken Campbell. Included by kind permission of United Agents Ltd on behalf of Daisy Campbell from the publication *Shell Connections 2006: New Plays for Young People* published by Faber and Faber Ltd, 2006.

Extract from *Fugee* by Abi Morgan. Included by kind permission of Abi Morgan from the publication *Shell Connections 2006: New Plays for Young People* published by Faber and Faber Ltd, 2006.

Extract from *My Face* by Nigel Williams. Included by kind permission of Nigel Williams from the publication *Shell Connections 2006: New Plays for Young People* published by Faber and Faber Ltd, 2006.

Extract from *Listen to Your Parents*, copyright © Benjamin Zephaniah, originally published in title *Theatre Centre Plays for Young People* Vol. 1 edited by Cheryl Robson. Included by kind permission of Aurora Metro Publications Ltd, London.

Extract from *Red Red Shoes*, copyright © Charles Way, originally published in title *Theatre Centre Plays for Young People*, Vol. 1 edited by Cheryl Robson. Included by kind permission of Aurora Metro Publications Ltd, London.

Extract from *Tin Soldier*, copyright © Noël Greig, originally published in title *Theatre Centre Plays for Young People*, Vol. 1 edited by Cheryl Robson. Included by kind permission of Aurora Metro Publications Ltd, London.

While the publishers have made every effort to contact copyright holders of material used in this volume, they would be grateful to hear from any they were unable to contact.

TEEP (Teacher Effectiveness Enhancement Programme) was developed by the Gatsby Charitable Foundation to support teachers to improve classroom practice and since its inception in 2002 has developed a variety of training models. Specialist Schools and Academies Trust became the host organisation in September 2010 and continue to nurture, grow and develop the programme. Visit www.ssatrust.org.uk/teep http://www.ssatrust.org.uk/teep to find out more.

Foreword

Playwriting and Young People

Playwriting has been going on for a long time. Twenty-five centuries ago, young Aeschylus started doing it in Greece; some time before the Seventh Century CE Kālidāsa wrote classic Sanskrit drama; then about a thousand years later Shakespeare turned up in London to discover there was work available for someone who hadn't been to university but could tell stories for the stage. But are the art and craft of playwriting now merely historical curiosities, utterly remote from the interests and concerns of people growing up at the start of the twenty-first century?

Playwriting uses words, when most societies on earth are dominated by the visual. Playwriting is realised in live performance: a communal experience in shared physical space, when our experience of the rest of the world is increasingly remote or solitary. Playwriting takes the conscious and unconscious outpourings of a single consciousness and embodies it to a group of other people, when elsewhere the boundaries between author and audience are dissolving in hypermediated interactivity. It can never be a truly mass medium, since the architectural limits of performance space and the biology of human sensory equipment restrict how many can see or hear at any time, just as they did in Aeschylus's Greece. The fleeting uniqueness of any performance moment makes it hard to commodify and package for commercial profit, particularly since the realisation of the playwright's art and craft requires time-consuming, labour-intensive preparation by a group employing a large range of physical and mental talents. Playwriting is 'slow' not 'fast', and hardly cost-effective when real people are prepared to play out true-life dramas at bargain rates on any channel at any time. Is playwriting irrelevant alongside Facebook and *The Apprentice*? Don't social media and reality television offer all of us the contemporary equivalent of what Aeschylus, Kālidāsa and Shakespeare were doing?

This book, and all the experience which has gone into writing it, suggest otherwise. Far from being a hopelessly out-dated form with nothing to offer, playwriting remains a powerful tool for both hearts and minds. What Caroline Jester and Claire Stoneman have distilled from years working with young people in diverse settings is a handbook which shares essentials from the art and craft of playwriting as widely as possible.

'Know thyself' was the advice carved on Apollo's Temple at Delphi, and playwriting demands no less. The first resource from which the playwright (of any age) draws is her or his own understanding, emotional capacity and imagination. The exercises in this book demand self-knowledge in different ways, consciously and unconsciously. All characters have something of their author in them: in creating fictional beings who face the world and its problems and possibilities, playwrights have the chance to enact alternatives (good, bad and morally indeterminate) like cosmic puppeteers. The swaggering lad for whom nothing apparently matters writes a tentative romantic encounter. The meek girl who never puts up her hand launches a ferocious diatribe against domestic restrictions. You can't write a good scene without putting something of yourself in there – even if only you know where that is. And sometimes even the writer doesn't see it until much later. It's not about self-exposure, nor the marketing of a saleable façade. It's you and it's not you at the same time, a liberating mask. The first time actors get up and perform scenes back to new playwrights, the blinking eyes and often nervous laughter of the writers register their shock and excitement as what was previously just inside their heads surprises them with its power in physical and vocal form.

Effective playwriting also demands empathy. You need to get inside more than one character's psyche, and this can be the most challenging, yet the most thrilling part of the task. You know what the character who wants to triumph over her bullies wants. You know the fury in the son's righteous outrage against his elders' hypocrisy. But you also have to write the *other side*. You have to be inside the bully too. You have to be that controlling parent as well. Your drama comes from you making them struggle. And the drama gets better, the deeper you dig in to both sides.

It's about quality, not quantity - whether it is a fragment of a scene that really takes off, or a single monologue, doesn't matter, as long as the playwright gets to feel the power of what the craft can do. Not everyone needs to be Aeschylus, Kālidāsa or Shakespeare. But when you do come across their works, and that of the many other playwrights whose work nourishes our collective culture, the act of having written drama yourself gives you new perspectives on their craft. I don't see playwriting simply as a tool to understand drama better on the page or the stage. But it's certainly a side effect that it gives new insights, particularly if young people get the chance (and why shouldn't they?) to see a range of contemporary drama on stage.

For the rest of us, the value of work like Jester and Stoneman's may be even more profound. It sows the seeds for a future dramatic repertoire which reflects the widest possible range of experience. No-one can predict which of the young people who come into contact with the inspirations in this book will go on to write terrific plays. But some of them will. And by widening the range of people who have access to this ancient, but also very modern, craft, the authors do us all a huge service. As will you, by taking it to your students.

Carl Miller

1

How to use the book

The book is arranged into six schemes of work (SoW) – a collection of sequenced lesson or session plans for the delivery of playwriting across the curriculum: Core SoW, SEN (Special Educational Needs) SoW, EAL (English as an Additional Language) SoW, Citizenship and Community SoW, PSHE (Personal, Social and Health Education) SoW and Moving beyond the KS3 curriculum: connecting with a qualification SoW. In each SoW there is an introduction, which includes a case study where relevant, the TEEP (Teacher Effectiveness Enhancement Programme) lesson plans and a resources section. Within the first two SoW (Core and SEN SoW), English teachers following the National Curriculum have the opportunity to assess writing, reading, listening and speaking skills through APP (Assessing Pupil Progress). AFs (Assessment Focuses) for each appropriate skill have been identified in every lesson. The EAL SoW does not follow APP but does incorporate a listening assessment linked to the acquisition of vocabulary for learners of English as an additional language. The Citizenship and Community SoW and PSHE SoW do not use APP as they are not part of the English curriculum, but English teachers could use the SoW as part of APP should they want to collaborate in cross-curricular work with teachers of these subject areas. The sixth SoW enables teachers following the Creative Writing Unit of Step Up (Skills Towards Enabling Progression) for adult literacy to assess student progress. This does not preclude anyone not following this curriculum or outside of an educational context using these SoW.

We recommend reading the Core SoW to introduce you in more detail to the building blocks of playwriting and then selecting the SoW that connects with the needs of your group and the requirements of the project. All of the extracts that are included, apart from examples from students, are published. We strongly suggest purchasing the full copies of these plays to develop this work further. Reading lists are included in the appendix.

For further information about APP (Assessing Pupil Progress) and the AF (Assessment Foci) for English, please see:

http://nationalstrategies.standards.dcsf.gov.uk/node/16051

It is important to note that at the time of writing, the current Conservative-Liberal Democrat government has yet to indicate whether it will make changes to APP in English, introduced by the Labour government in 2007.

Frequent abbreviations used throughout the book include:

AF   (Assessment Foci)

APP   (Assessing Pupil Progress)

AQA   examination board (Assessment and Qualifications Alliance)

CCEA   examination board (Council for the Curriculum, Examinations and Assessment)

Core   (Core Scheme of Work aimed at Key Stage 3 English students)

EAL   (English as an Additional Language)

KS3   (Key Stage 3 – students aged 11–14 years)

OCR   examination board (Oxford, Cambridge and Royal Society of Arts)

OFSTED (Office for Standards in Education)

PLTS   (Personal, Learning and Thinking Skills)

PSHE   (Personal, Social and Health Education)

SEN   (Special Educational Needs)

SoW   (Schemes of Work)

TEEP   (Teacher Effectiveness Enhancement Programme)

WJEC   examination board (Welsh Joint Education Committee)

Introduction

Playwriting has been seen as something of a mystery for too long. Playwrights are, in some eyes, the alchemists of theatre, writing plays using their secret formula. This school of thought believe that there is no methodology to the teaching of playwriting and question how you can teach it. Whilst we agree that masters of any craft go beyond methodologies and subvert the rules leading audiences into new realms, we have witnessed the demystification of this art form within classrooms. The results have not only improved literacy levels but also helped to develop personal, social and creative expression. This book aims to be used as a way of introducing the teaching of playwriting into the classroom and to give every student the opportunity, regardless of barriers to learning, to engage with this art form by writing their own plays.

The teaching of playwriting in the UK

In 1989 David Edgar, one of the most prolific dramatists of the post-1960s generation in Great Britain, set up the first MA, now MPhil in Playwriting at Birmingham University. This course initially raised questions about whether there should be such courses:

> From the beginning, we were up against the British cult of the crusty amateur: that prejudice which, in the theatre, is expressed in the belief that while actors can benefit from training (along with stage managers and other footsoldiers of the craft), directors and writers are supposed to acquire their skills telepathically; that the very idea of training devalues the status and may indeed stunt the imagination of the lone artist engaged in isolated struggle with the muse.
>
> (*How Plays Work* by David Edgar, p. xii)

The results, however, can not only be found in a list of writers who regularly have their work produced on stages across the world (Steve Waters, Sarah Kane, Sarah Woods, Fraser Grace, Charles Mulekwa, Stephanie Dale, Anthony Weigh to name but a few) but it has also generated what could be described as a quiet revolution, with many courses now teaching playwriting in higher education establishments across the United Kingdom. With this book, we hope to knock on the doors of secondary educators and find a way into revealing 'the mystery' at an age when students are making independent choices. This could result in not only enhancing their writing and communication skills, but igniting their interest in theatre, creating the next generation of theatregoers, and maybe a few award-winning playwrights along the way.

Young writers' programmes have existed in theatres where playwrights pass on their skills to younger artists and often go into schools to deliver playwriting programmes. We aim to equip the teacher and workshop leader with the skills to deliver these programmes so that they can become embedded within the core curriculum and not be merely bolt-on extra-curricular activities. Our work over the last decade has demonstrated that the tools of playwriting can be beneficial in developing literacy and personal and social skills and that the 'formula' we have used does not exclude any student. This book has a strong focus on Key Stage 3 (KS3, students aged 11–14 years – although more and more schools are shortening KS3 and beginning KS4 in year 9 now) because of its freedom, outside the pressure of exams, to apply this work through various schemes of work (SoW). There are also SoW within this book that can be easily adapted across the curriculum. Our ambition is that this work will become common practice and find its own route into the next act that leads it to connect with qualifications in secondary education.

The schemes of work within this book

The schemes of work (SoW) within this book have been developed over a number of years and tried and tested with students of all abilities. Students who are high academic achievers, students with special educational needs (SEN), students with English as an additional language (EAL) and students outside mainstream education are just some who have written their own plays as a result of these schemes. It is our ambition to equip the teacher with a basic toolkit to deliver playwriting programmes with students of wide-ranging abilities. The fundamentals of playwriting are explored in each SoW and adapted for the different needs within each group.

Previously, anything to do with theatre has been mostly taught through Drama courses, but we believe every student should have access to this work via English lessons, as the focus of this book is on the craft of *writing*. The book comprises a Core SoW aimed at Key Stage 3 students (11–14-year=olds) and five other models where playwriting has proven to be a powerful tool in student development and engagement. Models for students with special educational needs (SEN), with English as an additional language (EAL), schemes for Citizenship and Community projects, a "Play in a Day" scheme that explores elements of emotional literacy and Personal, Social and Health Education (PSHE) have been included.

Also included is a scheme for adult literacy, based on the Creative Writing unit of the 'Step Up' (Skills Towards Enabling Progression) qualification through the National Open College Network. Through this SoW, students can include the work developed for their portfolios towards this qualification, where the outcomes are based on the National Adult Literacy Curriculum. It is our ambition that this SoW will highlight how playwriting can become embedded within the curriculum and connect with qualifications.

The Citizenship and Community SoW can cross over into other areas of the curriculum including sociology, history and geography. We also include ideas for how playwriting can be introduced digitally to help to promote international collaborations in the final section of the book.

All of the SoW in the book, with the exception of the Citizenship and Community SoW, identify the Personal, Learning and Thinking Skills (PLTS) that are addressed in the lessons. The PLTS emerged in the new National Curriculum of 2008 after first appearing in a 2005 14–19 White Paper. They were put forward by the then Labour government as a framework of skills for learning in school, at home and in the world of work. The PLTS are outlined as the following: independent enquiry; creative thinking; reflective learning; teamwork; self-management and effective participation. Many English schools have embedded the teaching of these skills into their curriculum. We have identified in the lessons the PLTS that are addressed; teachers and workshop leaders may be able to explicitly teach more of them in the SoW, should they so wish. We have not identified the PLTS in the Citizenship and Community SoW as the focus was very much on emotional literacy and feelings. However, teachers and workshop leaders are encouraged to teach the PLTS within this SoW if they wish to. At the time of writing this book the coalition Conservative-Liberal Democrat government have not made any changes as yet to the PLTS framework, but are conducting a review of the secondary National Curriculum.

How to assess students' playwriting

It is important to note that although this book has been written with teachers and workshop leaders from schools, theatres and other groups in mind, it is also a tool for secondary school English teachers from state schools to assess students' reading, writing, and speaking and listening using Assessing Pupil Progress (APP). APP is a structured approach to student assessment in English so that teachers can track students' progress in reading and writing through Key Stage 3 and use diagnostic information about students' strengths and weaknesses.

Based on the assessment focuses (AFs) that underpin National Curriculum assessment, the approach aims to improve the quality and reliability of teachers' assessment and provide a holistic picture of each student's attainment, rather than relying on a test at the end of a topic.

APP is straightforward and is used in a number of different curriculum areas. At regular intervals, which are planned to fit in with a departmental and whole-school assessment policy, teachers review students' work using the APP guidelines to build a profile of their attainment. The information gained from this allows teachers to analyse the strengths and weaknesses of each student in reading, writing, speaking and listening and assign each pupil an overall National Curriculum level for those skills. This information is then used to set curricular targets to extend students' learning, and is also used to inform future teaching.

English teachers using APP generally keep an assessment folder or portfolio of how students are progressing in reading, writing, speaking and listening. Each area is also sub-divided into assessment focuses (AFs). Assessed work can be kept in portfolios, but evidence of attainment is also sourced in exercise books used in class and as part of homework. Each school that uses APP manages it in different ways.

Our aim was not to focus the Core and SEN SoW solely on APP. Rather, we aim to support APP in secondary state schools by providing opportunities throughout the SoW for teachers, should they wish, to gather evidence of students' ability in reading, writing, speaking and listening to add to their portfolio of evidence as to how each student is progressing in each area. Points throughout the Core and SEN SoW have been identified where students can demonstrate their skills in different APP assessment focuses (AFs) in reading, writing, and speaking and listening. APP will be very familiar to many English teachers, and we hope that the Core and SEN lesson plans will help to illustrate how the analysis of plays and playwriting can be used to enhance students' ability in some of the assessment focuses. The SEN lessons also refer to the P scales – assessment criteria to help assess students with special educational needs working below level 1 on the Assessment Focuses of APP. This is to assist teachers and workshop leaders in both mainstream and special schools to assess students' writing using the P scales; the strategies included in the SEN SoW facilitate 'writing' in a number of different ways. The use of APP and the P scales does not in any way preclude the lesson plans from being used in schools that do not use APP or the P scales, such as UK independent schools or schools in other countries.

How to use the schemes of work in schools and theatre projects

We use the term scheme of work (SoW) to indicate a group of lesson plans with clear learning objectives, points of assessment and a linear 'thread' of learning, and accompanying resources. We are aware that different schools have different interpretations of what SoW are, what they look like and how they function. We strongly encourage schools to adapt the SoW in this book to their own approaches to short-, medium- and long-term planning in English to enable the best outcomes possible for their students and to embed playwriting into the curriculum. We aim to provide a framework for teaching playwriting across the curriculum, not a rigid structure.

We have stipulated timings only in the Core and Personal, Social and Health Education (PSHE) SoW, based around a 70-minute lesson. Other SoW do not have timings indicated, as these SoW are tailored to specific groups of learners and the SoW may be taught differently within the curriculum in school in terms of allocated time. We wanted to ensure that schools and theatres felt that these SoW were as flexible as possible and that they could adapt timings according to the needs of the students.

Whilst the emphasis is on making the connections between playwriting and the classroom, this book is by no means exclusive to educational establishments. Theatres could introduce these SoWs into many areas of community engagement work, using playwriting as a means of generating creative responses to projects and productions and generating new audiences. The Citizenship and Community SoW offers opportunities to connect groups who would not normally have the chance to collaborate, and there is enough freedom within them to select topics and events that have significant local, national or international meanings to various communities. Projects that have an historical focus would work well, offering cross-generational debate through this creative outlet. The English as an additional language (EAL) SoW also offers avenues into engaging with newer communities who may not be connecting with the work on the stage because of language barriers. This also allows a two-way dialogue to emerge and has opportunities to explore new commissioning and programming ideas. Other groups and workshop leaders will find this work useful in instigating projects, including youth groups, play schemes and many more. The SoW use the term 'teacher' for the purpose of continuity but this can mean workshop leader and/or practitioner.

What led to the development of this playwriting model?

The idea for this work has developed over ten years and was initiated by the Birmingham Repertory Theatre's young writers' programme, 'Transmissions'. In 1998 the theatre's studio space was renamed The Door and became dedicated to new writing. At this time 'Transmissions' was born to develop plays by young writers aged 12–25 years. Playwrights Noël Greig and Carl Miller delivered playwriting workshops, and an award-winning model was born. A desire to widen the access to this work began with an outreach programme, 'Transmissions in Schools', to deliver playwriting programmes in schools and pupil referral units (PRUs). Playwrights delivered these based upon the core programme at the theatre. Teachers were offered a day's training to understand the basics of teaching playwriting, with the aim that they would incorporate this into their own practice after the programme had finished.

Schools began to recognise how powerful this model was and started to develop their own schemes of work. So the idea to design a model that included the requirements of the curriculum within the Key Stage 3 (KS3) National Curriculum for English was born. Within the Key Stage 3 (11–14-year-olds – but some schools are shortening Key Stage 3 to end at the end of year 8) National Curriculum for English, three strands are taught: reading, writing, and speaking and listening. The teaching of plays and drama in English has always traditionally been within the domain of reading skills (the analysis of characters; language; dramatic devices and structures etc.) and speaking and listening with the proverbial role-plays and hot-seating activities. Whilst this is vital, what was missing was the teaching of the craft of playwriting as a *writing* skill. When teaching plays, teachers would sometimes include a 'Now write a new scene for the play' activity or 'Write your own play on a similar theme' without knowing explicitly how to teach this. The teaching of playwriting has not historically been included in any teacher training of new English teachers on PGCE (Postgraduate Certificate of Education) courses or similar. A fresh new approach was needed.

Key Stage 3 was the most obvious entrance due to the lack of exam pressure. English department curriculum and faculty leaders were asked whether this was something they would welcome and they replied with a unanimous yes, stating that it was simply a lack of experience in this area that stopped teachers already doing this. Plays are obviously already taught in schools as part of reading and speaking and listening work, but research proved that these were mostly older texts. What was lacking was the connection between the new writing that was being seen on British stages and what was being taught in the classroom. This book offers a way into addressing both of these gaps: providing teachers with an insight into teaching playwriting in the classroom and students with the opportunity to study contemporary plays that hopefully resonate with their experiences and widen their worlds. Whilst the focus of the Core SoW is Key Stage 3, there is versatility to this work, and the English as an additional language (EAL) and Citizenship and Community SoW will almost certainly cross into Key Stages 4 and 5.

The extracts used throughout the book

Our aim is to introduce a new canon of plays into the classroom that connect with the explosion of new theatre writing that has taken place over the last two decades. We have included extracts from work that has been published to enable teachers to purchase the full scripts and take this work further if they wish. Examples of students' work are also included within the SoWs to illustrate what can be achieved with students of very differing abilities.

The extracts that we have selected for this book are from some of the most exciting voices within contemporary British theatre. There are several suggested extracts in some lesson plans to reflect the rich and varied voices that can be found on our stages and within the classrooms.

Many of the selected plays have been taken from the National Theatre's New Connections programme. New Connections gives young companies nationwide the chance to perform new plays by established contemporary playwrights. This work has already transcended the barriers between work for, by and with young people, with some plays crossing into The National's main repertoire (*Chatroom* by Enda Walsh, *Burn* by Deborah Gearing and *Citizenship* by Mark Ravenhill). Dennis Kelly's play *Deoxyribonucleic Acid (DNA)* is now a GCSE text and copies of the plays in the Connections series, published by Faber and Faber, have been placed in every secondary school in the United Kingdom. We have discovered that many teachers are unaware that this resource is already in their library.

Extracts from Fin Kennedy's exciting work with Mulberry School in Tower Hamlets, London, are also used and offer an insight into the potential for collaboration between playwrights, students and playwriting. Since 2006, Mulberry School has Specialist Arts status and Fin has been playwright-in-residence, running courses for students and teachers alike and creating 'The Edinburgh Festival Project', a play that he writes in collaboration with the students. These plays are performed by the company and have received critical acclaim, with 'The Unravelling' being awarded a Fringe First. An anthology of these plays has been published by Nick Hern Books: *The Urban Girl's Guide to Camping and other plays*. Fin's ideas for these plays come from workshops with the students; 'My writing takes its cue from the corridors of Mulberry School itself' (*The Urban Girl's Guide to Camping and other plays*, p. x).

Theatre Centre commissions, produces and tours work for younger audiences, and this work is increasingly being published. Theatre Centre is one of the country's leading touring companies for young audiences, and aims: 'to empower the voices and raise the aspirations of young people, teachers and writers through the process of creating and experiencing professional theatre' (Theatre Centre website) and we hope the extracts we have included from their anthology *Theatre Centre Plays for Young People* (Aurora Metro Publications) goes some way to realising their vision.

Unicorn Theatre was the first children's theatre company to gain national recognition and now has the only purpose-built theatre for young people in central London. The company commissions and produces extraordinary work that challenges our perceptions of what younger audiences should see. Much of this work, unfortunately, is not published, which is a great shame for audiences across the country that cannot make it to this incredible venue. The award-winning *Red Red Shoes* by prolific writer Charles Way is published and was commissioned by Unicorn Theatre; it offers a glimpse of the gems we are missing by not publishing this work. *Class Acts* is a programme run by Unicorn to commission new writers to write plays for Year 6 students to perform, and an anthology of three plays by writers Oladipo Agboluaje, Lin Coghlan and Philip Osment is published by Oberon. These would make excellent examples in a transitional playwriting programme for Year 6 and Year 7 students in the Citizenship and Community SoW.

Regional theatres produce much new work, and *The Mother Ship* by Douglas Maxwell, commissioned and produced by Birmingham Repertory Theatre (an extract from which is included in this book), won the prestigious Brian Way Award for theatre for younger audiences. We were unable to include all of the extracts we wanted to in this book, and therefore make reference to three published plays in the Citizenship and Community SoW that would work well: *One Night in November* by Alan Pollock, commissioned and produced by Belgrade Theatre Coventry; *The Day the Waters Came* by Lisa Evans, commissioned and produced by Theatre Centre; and *Ostrich Boys*, adapted by Carl Miller from the novel by Keith Gray, commissioned and produced by Birmingham Repertory Theatre.

Published plays aimed at audiences under 11 (and, for the purposes of this book, students working below a reading age of 11) are limited. Noël Greig, a playwright who wrote a number of plays for young people and children, worked with Tangere Arts to produce three plays that can be found in the timely publication *Tin Soldier and other plays for children* (Aurora Metro Publications). All three of the plays in this anthology contain rich material that could be adapted for secondary students with lower reading ages, for example they could be used in the lesson plans in the SEN SoW.

By no means is this meant to be an exhaustive list of work for younger audiences, but it is intended to demonstrate the diverse work that does exist and to make connections between educators and theatres. On a national level little new work is being commissioned and produced for audiences aged 11–14 years, and a dialogue with this audience through their own generation of ideas via playwriting could go some way to bridge this gap by listening to what excites young people of this age. There is a wealth of other media aimed at this age group, and writer development programmes in theatre companies such as Unicorn, the Birmingham Repertory Theatre and Half Moon are exploring this area on the stage.

Examples of students' scripts have also been included throughout the book as case studies and to be used in some lessons. Please note that spelling, punctuation and grammatical errors have not been corrected. The students' scripts are unedited and are exactly how they were written in order to preserve the authenticity and integrity of their writing. Some of these 'errors' are deliberate and have been included so that words and sentences are read in specific ways.

TEEP (Teacher Effectiveness Enhancement Programme)

Our aim is to introduce a new canon of plays into the classroom and to empower teachers and theatre practitioners to be able to teach playwriting to young people. To enable teachers and theatre practitioners to 'hang' the teaching of playwriting onto a flexible framework rather than a rigid structure, the Teacher Effectiveness Enhancement Programme (TEEP) was chosen after some years developing the teaching of playwriting using the TEEP framework with schools in the United Kingdom. In 2006, when the playwriting model using TEEP was in developmental stages, two lessons from the model were taught at Kelly High School, Chicago, as part of the students' ongoing work on playwriting and scripts. The students, many of whom spoke English as a second language, engaged brilliantly with the writing strategies in the lessons. Furthermore, the fast-paced, carefully constructed nature of learning within the TEEP lessons led to excellent student engagement and progress within the lessons. TEEP's appeal, therefore, is also its universality of application. It can be used successfully in a variety of contexts, as our case studies show.

TEEP was developed in 2002. Prior to its development, the early noughties saw the emergence of a number of different 'learning models', particularly in secondary education. Teachers were structuring lessons into the learning experience of a 'starter' (introductory activity at the start of a lesson), 'main' (the main body of the lesson) and 'plenary' (the concluding activity of the lesson), but it was felt that something new was needed, grounded in outstanding teaching and learning and improving classroom practice. TEEP emerged in 2002, led by the Gatsby Foundation as an action research programme to support teachers to improve their pedagogy. The model was developed originally for training of STEM subjects (science; technology; engineering; mathematics) but has proved successful for teachers of any subject area and in all sectors of education. Since 2002 the programme has grown in numbers of staff trained and the variety of training approaches offered to learning institutions.

TEEP has been key in supporting individual teachers, trainee teachers, departments, whole schools, groups of schools and local authorities to improve classroom practice. It is a proven learning model which focuses on effective learner and teacher behaviours, underpinned by the five key elements of thinking for learning, accelerated learning, assessment for learning, collaborative learning and the effective use of ICT. These underpinning elements act as a means by which learning is transmitted, with outstanding teaching and learning demonstrated by teacher and student.

This outstanding teaching and learning is exemplified in the TEEP learning cycle (adapted from the Cramlington learning cycle) a guide used by teachers to plan meaningful and stimulating lessons. The cycle is intended to provide a strategic and cohesive approach to planning lessons, and does not necessarily follow a linear path. Teachers use their professional judgement to move backwards and forwards throughout the cycle to best meet the needs of their students.

Independent research evaluations of TEEP have been carried out by Warwick University, York University and the London Institute of Education, all highlighting its benefits. All three reports conclude that the training positively affected the way teachers behaved in the classroom. They describe increased engagement of students in their learning, improved behaviour in lessons, increase in active learning by students, increase in higher-level thinking and improved attainment. TEEP's impact has also been recognised in a number of successful Ofsted inspections around the UK.

As of 1 September 2010 the Specialist Schools and Academies Trust (SSAT) became the custodians of the Teacher Effectiveness Enhancement Programme (TEEP), further raising the profile of the programme.

How to use the TEEP cycle

The TEEP cycle promotes the teacher's metacognitive thought processes, the 'thinking about thinking', behind the reasons for choosing specific activities in lessons and the impact they will have on students' thinking and learning. It structures the learning through building blocked phases of the lesson, as follows:

1. Prepare for Learning

This is the first phase of the lesson and really 'sets the scene' for learning and a climate that is conducive to learning. It is important for the teacher to consider in this phase how the new learning connects with prior learning. It is also vital for the teacher to consider the emotional and physical environment. The students need to be 'hooked' into their learning from the outset. All the SoWs in this book include Prepare for Learning activities that promote thinking and connecting the learning, which is moving far beyond a traditional 'starter' activity. It is not just about 'starting' the lesson, but is about connecting with the learning in the bigger picture, and sharing this with the students.

2. Agree the Learning Objectives/Learning Outcomes

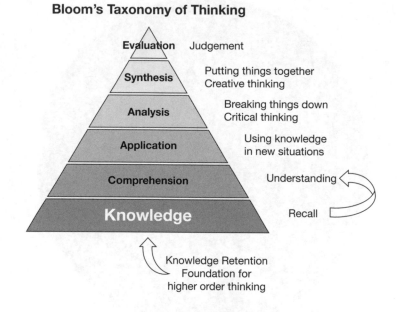

Bloom's Taxonomy of Thinking

- Evaluation — Judgement
- Synthesis — Putting things together / Creative thinking
- Analysis — Breaking things down / Critical thinking
- Application — Using knowledge in new situations
- Comprehension — Understanding
- Knowledge — Recall

Knowledge Retention
Foundation for
higher order thinking

The second phase of the lesson is vital so that the purpose of learning is shared with the students. In this book, other than the final SoW which is linked to the learning outcomes of a specific qualification, we only outline learning objectives as opposed to learning outcomes. Schools have differing approaches to learning objectives and learning outcomes, and we have left it open for schools to identify their own learning outcomes for each lesson. We have, however, provided learning objectives as a guide to teachers to demonstrate how learning about playwriting can easily become embedded into the curriculum. We recommend that teachers map progress through the different levels of Bloom's Taxonomy of thinking – enabling students, through learning about playwriting, to progress from knowledge and understanding right through to the higher-level thinking skills of synthesis and evaluation. We have provided learning objectives in the lesson plans that clearly show this progression at different points for all students, regardless of ability.

3. Present New Information through the Senses

This phase enables the teacher to consider other, inventive ways of presenting new information to the students to arouse their curiosity and promote their engagement with the learning, catering for different learning styles of visual, auditory and kinaesthetic. For example, in the Core SoW lesson 2, students are provided with different stimuli of pictures, photographs and music to prompt thoughts and questions as ideas for their emerging stories. In lesson 2 of the EAL SoW a world map is presented to the group, along with the silhouette of a person – the main character for the play. The students are encouraged to literally map out where this main character is going from country to country on the map, providing the narrative structure for the play. The teacher then records information about the main character and the list of countries the students identify; these become the locations for the play.

4. Construct

This phase of the lesson is where the students are given time to process and actively construct this new learning. Students often work in groups in this phase on collaborative thinking, but individual work is equally valid. This phase of the lesson is where students try things out, make errors and process new ideas. For example, in the Construct phase of lesson 3 of the EAL SoW, students are working as a group to write a scene in a specific location, building confidence before applying this new learning to their individual and smaller-group work in the Apply to Demonstrate phase of the lesson.

5. Apply to Demonstrate New Understanding

Students now apply their new learning in this phase of the lesson, demonstrating their understanding. This can be in a variety of ways – through writing, speaking, drawing, performing, creating etc. In lesson 3 of the SEN SoW we had to plan other ways for students who could not write to 'write' about their characters and the location of their play. In this phase of the lesson the students are provided with other ways to demonstrate their learning and ideas – through sculpture, drawing or collage. Signs and symbols can be added to the sculptures, drawing and collages to indicate further ideas about characters (e.g. symbol cards showing an emotion) or location (weather symbols etc.).

6. Review

This phase of the lesson is crucial in ensuring that new learning is embedded. Although it is seen as coming at the end of the lesson cycle, opportunities for regular review and engagement with the learning objectives should be integrated into lessons. The Review phase should encourage reflection not just on what has been learnt, but how it has been learnt and the thinking processes the students have gone through. Careful, open-ended questioning from the teacher is helpful here. In many of the SoW the Review phase is used to read and reflect on the scenes that have been written, and students are asked to consider various ideas in light of their learning about the development of their plays.

The TEEP cycle itself echoes the process of playwriting, the phases of the lesson reflecting the building blocks of a play, resembling one scene within the complete piece, one small unit of action along the learning journey. This is why TEEP is so powerful when used to structure the teaching of playwriting. It is also why it has had such a profound impact on the students and teachers who have experienced the TEEP-structured lessons in the work that has culminated in this book.

For further information about TEEP and TEEP training, please see www.teep.org.uk.

Ready to write plays

Noël Greig's pioneering work in this field has led the way to make playwriting an accessible art form that has huge potential for unearthing and unlocking creativity and personal expression in all students. His book *Playwriting: A Practical Guide*, which is referred to throughout, offers anyone embarking upon the teaching of playwriting in any context a wealth of material to engage students with. We hope this book retains some of his passion by focusing on secondary education and that his belief in the universality of the power of playwriting can be found within.

> The little scene written and performed in the classroom may pass off in an afternoon and never be heard of again. The new play written by one author and presented on the stage of a national theatre may pass into the canon of great, universal works. But as events that bring us together and connect us with each other they are equal.
>
> (Noël Greig, *Playwriting: A Practical Guide*, p. xiii)

A full set of downloadable PDF versions of the lesson plans and additional resources can be accessed, by buyers of this book, on the Routledge website. Please visit www.routledge.com/9780415590969 and click on the 'eResources' tab.

2

Core playwriting SoW

Introduction to Core SoW

This SoW is entitled 'Core' because it is the basis for all of the other programmes. It has been proven over the course of six years to work with multiple groups of different ages and abilities, ranging from secondary students working at National Curriculum level 1 and level 2 to students working at National Curriculum level 8 and predicted A* for GCSE English. The Core SoW has been taught in academically very high-achieving schools; in 'National Challenge' English schools achieving below 30% 5 A*–C including English and maths; in schools just emerging from Ofsted's 'Special Measures' category with students displaying very challenging behaviours; in Ofsted category 'Outstanding' schools; in inner-city schools; in huge single-sex schools; in new academies; in schools in areas with very high socio-economic deprivation. Taster lessons from the SoW have also been taught in a public school in inner-city Chicago, Illinois. It has been tried and tested by teachers and students and is the culmination of feedback and input from developmental work in all these rich and varied learning environments.

The Core SoW is designed for use within English lessons at KS3, with any year group in the key stage and any ability (although the SEN SoW would be more appropriate for students working at level 1 or below on the P scales). Different extracts have been included, some more challenging in vocabulary and content than others; teachers can decide which extracts would be most appropriate for their groups. It can therefore be taught to set groups of different ability or mixed-ability groups.

Although the SoW has primarily been designed to teach the craft of play*writing*, the SoW also offers English teachers the opportunity to assess reading and speaking and listening skills through APP – Assessing Pupil Progress; Assessment Focuses (AFs) for each of these areas have been identified in every lesson. This does not preclude the SoW being used by schools that do not follow the English National Curriculum. It does, however, enable schools that do follow the English National Curriculum to embed it within their tracking of students' learning in English as part of APP. At regular intervals in the lesson plans, teachers review students' work using the APP guidelines to build a profile of their attainment. These opportunities throughout the Core and SEN schemes of work enable teachers to gather evidence of students' ability in reading, writing, speaking and listening to add to their portfolio of evidence as to how each student is progressing in each area.

Every SoW in this book has been designed to incorporate the following 'basic ingredients' of playwriting, but the format has been adapted to the requirements of each group:

Finding stories

Stories are everywhere, and each SoW has a different approach to help the student find the story for their play. Inspiration for stories can be found in the world around us, the people we meet, past historical events, local events and many more places. Noël Greig's book *Playwriting: A Practical Guide* offers a wealth of material to explore this further if you wish.

Characters

Students will explore how to develop different characters and how these characters behave and inhabit different situations and react to each other. The emphasis in the SoW is to create complex characters with detailed histories.

Location/environment

The SoW pushes students to explore interesting locations where their characters live out their journeys, often resulting in the locations becoming characters in themselves by helping to move the narrative forward. The environment impacts upon the way a character behaves and the choices the student needs to make for their characters in certain situations.

Structure/timeframe

A variety of structures are included as examples within the Core SoW, which will hopefully enable the student to find the right structure for their play rather than imposing a rigid formula. The aim of the SoW is to free up the student's imagination and demystify the process of playwriting rather than impose a set of rules that must be adhered to. We also encourage English teachers to explore the notion of dramatic structures and devices with the students, terms more frequently used with students at KS4 in GCSE English Literature when studying drama. In lesson 7 of the SoW we provide examples of plays for students to read to analyse both dramatic structures and devices, and to apply these ideas to their own plays. We have suggested that teachers take some extra time to analyse dramatic structure and dramatic devices should they so wish.

Objectives and obstacles/deepening the story/dramatic action

All characters need an objective, a reason to be in the play that allows them to have their individual journeys. If a character does not have their own journey they could be seen as offering only a functional role within the play. The obstacles are the things that stand in the way of the characters attaining their objectives, and it is these obstacles that create the dramatic action within the play by making the character work harder to achieve their goals. The obstacles in the guise of another character reveal the subtext and information about the characters and their relationships, in addition to pushing the story forward and enabling the student to really deepen their narrative.

Workshop section

The majority of professionally commissioned writers will go through a 'workshop process' where their work is read by and explored with actors before the final draft is delivered to the theatre. All of the SoW include a workshop section to enable the students to experience this often crucial stage in a script's development, to try things out and see whether they are working. The other students will act as 'dramaturg' here, asking questions about the scripts that will hopefully lead and unlock something for the writer to develop further. This stage is not for others to criticise work, but to develop their analytical skills. They will have a dramatic vocabulary in relation to their own writing to use by this stage.

Rewriting

Writing is rewriting, and this may be something that teachers feel they wish to develop further within the SoW. The workshop section will raise many new things that the students will wish to change or start, and time should be given to ensure that this is explored as a crucial stage in re-evaluating their own plays.

The lesson plans are not prescriptive but are a recommended path to teaching playwriting within English lessons at KS3. They are flexible, working documents that teachers will need to personalise and differentiate to the needs of their own groups. We strongly recommend that teachers use the lesson plans alongside their own schools' lesson planning guidance and enrich the lesson plans, as good teachers do, with their own inspirational ideas and strategies.

Examples of texts to use

The Core SoW is designed for individual students to be introduced to playwriting by a series of writing strategies that build and deepen their stories and characters' journeys along the way. Extracts of plays by some of the UK's leading contemporary playwrights have been included to help demonstrate the application of the writing skills being explored. The inclusion of this work is also to begin to introduce a new canon of plays into the English curriculum that has been written in recent years and makes the connection with new work seen on British stages. An extended reading list is provided and all of these plays are easily available from various publishers. A copy of the 'Connections' plays for each year, which were developed at the National Theatre, should already be in every secondary school in the UK, published by Faber and Faber. One of the writing strategies in lesson 2 asks the student to prepare a speech to receive a national playwriting award. Many of the playwrights included in the SoW are award-winning writers, and teachers could use these contemporary playwrights as examples. Roy Williams (OBE 2008) for example, whose play *Baby Girl* is mentioned in lesson 1, has won many awards, including Evening Standard Award for Most Promising Playwright, BAFTA Award for Best Schools Drama for *Offside* in 2002, and South Bank Show Arts Council Decibel Award 2004.

Lesson 1 offers teachers an immediate way in to exploring what makes a play a play and not another form of drama or fiction. It begins to focus the students' thinking about why their story should be told in this medium and not another. The use of Fin Kennedy's verse drama in *Stolen Secrets* opens the discussion about what theatre is: action that happens in the present. There is a tendency for students to imitate what they see and hear around them from other media, such as television drama and Hollywood films. This lesson immediately separates these by exploring conflict in the present, which is at the heart of any good live drama.

All four of the extracts in lesson 1, in the Construct section, demonstrate conflict at the start of a scene. *Make 'n' Mend* and *Baby Girl* open with mother–daughter disagreements, with *My Face* showing the character's internal conflict with the way she views her body and the reality of how she looks to others. *Listen to Your Parents* sets up the conflict of the character, as his dichotomy is how football and poetry can coexist. The students then apply this understanding to their own writing, and *Cheesy Feet Man and the Disaster*, written by Tyran Jones, a Year 8 student, can also be used to demonstrate this. At the time of starting the playwriting SoW, Tyran was working at level 3 of the National Curriculum for English.

To enable students to get a sense of the different styles and techniques they can apply to their own plays, we would recommend reading all three extracts in lesson 3.

The extracts in lesson 4 illustrate the importance of individual speech patterns, and the way a character chooses to speak tells us a lot about what is going on in that character's world. In *The Mothership*, the character of Kevin is in the process of inventing his own language, his own way of not swearing, to show the world that he has changed and is different to how others perceive him.

We have also included examples of students' work in lesson 5 from Shenley Academy (then Shenley Court School). These Year 8 students were working at level 2 or level 3 of the National Curriculum for English when they started playwriting SoW. All three of them applied conflict at the beginning of their own scenes and go straight into the action, avoiding the need for exposition.

We actively encourage teachers to promote students' independent research throughout the SoW. This is a natural part of the writing process, especially when students are exploring worlds and characters outside of their immediate environments, potentially in different social, cultural or historical contexts.

Research and inspiration can come from anywhere, and a way in to developing ideas about character and starting points for the students' plays is explored in the Review phase of lesson 3 through the use of digital media. Students are directed to researching publicly viewable status updates and Tweets. These can be used as a starting point for the students to create a character around that line of information and can generate a number of questions, thoughts and ideas. For example, what sort of character could this be? What can we infer from this status update/ Tweet about this person? How does this person speak? What do we learn about them from the way they speak? The status updates/Tweets could even become the first lines of the students' plays. This idea was inspired by the London Wall Thomson and Craighead exhibition at the Museum of London in 2010, where social networking traffic from within a three-mile radius of the Museum of London was displayed as a vast array of typeset posters revealing what London people felt, thought and did over a 10-hour snapshot in time.

The SoW inherently raises questions about dramatic structure throughout, but does ask the student to reflect upon this. We hope that the application of this work will not inhibit the individual student in expressing themselves and is not too formulaic. There are a number of excellent books about playwriting if you wish to explore this in more detail, and these are on the suggested reading list.

Lesson plans, resources and extracts for Core SoW

Lesson 1 (Page 32)

Resources

- Range of text types – poetry, narrative, different types of non-fiction etc.
- Sticky notes
- Sign saying 'Question Wall' and designated space in room where students can post sticky notes with thoughts, questions and queries about their learning
- Extracts (in resources) from:
  ◊ 'Make 'n' Mend' *from Stolen Secrets*
  ◊ *Baby Girl*
  ◊ *My Face*
  ◊ *Listen to Your Parents*
  ◊ *Cheesy Feet Man and the Disaster*

Lesson 2 (Page 40)

Resources

- Varied mix of photos/images that show different views from around the world and different cultures, situations, contexts etc.
- Sticky notes
- Evocative music for students to listen to (e.g. 'Mars' from Holst's *The Planets Suite*)
- Video clip of an after-dinner speaker

Lesson 3 (Page 41)

Resources

- Sticky notes
- Extracts (in resources) from:
  - ◊ *School Journey to the Centre of the Earth*
  - ◊ 'Not a Girl' from *Stolen Secrets*
- Computers with access to the internet and Facebook/Twitter

Lesson 4 (Page 47)

Resources

Image of a suitcase or bag and its contents or a real suitcase or bag with contents. The contents need to be thought-provoking and be a stimulus for the students to think about the character that owns the suitcase

- Flipchart (if possible)
- Character History Sheet
- Sticky notes
- Extracts (in resources) from:
  - ◊ *Listen to Your Parents*
  - ◊ *Fugee*
  - ◊ *The Mother Ship*

Lesson 5 (Page 54)

Resources

- Extract (in resource) from *The Miracle*
- Extracts (in resources) from plays written by students at Shenley Academy
  - ◊ *Theme Park*
  - ◊ *Aliens from Mars*
  - ◊ *Football Match*

Lesson 6 (Page 59)

Resources

- Sticky notes
- Photos/images of different locations – e.g. train station, library, hospital ward, car park, shopping centre, airport, park, school corridor, the moon etc.

Lesson 7 (Page 60)

Resources

- Washing line/string
- Different sized pieces of paper or card 'pegged' up on the line (alternatively you could have real items of clothing on the line!)
- For analysing dramatic structure and dramatic devices the following extracts from within the book could be used:
  ◊ The chorus as a character in itself, helping to push the story forward – *Stolen Secrets; Red Red Shoes* (see Core SoW resources lesson 8)
  ◊ The use of monologues to explore multiple realities and worlds within a play, but still active and in the present, not reflective – *My Face; Listen to Your Parents; The Urban Girl's Guide to Camping*
  ◊ Symbolic objects – *Red Red Shoes;* 'Make 'n' Mend' *(Stolen Secrets); The Miracle; Fugee; The Urban Girl's Guide to Camping*
  ◊ Repetition of scenes and repeated linguistic riffs – *My Face*
  ◊ Characters 'creating' the world of the play – *School Journey to the Centre of the Earth*
  ◊ In *School Journey to the Centre of the Earth* the characters physicalise different events that they think might happen – e.g. the rollercoaster.

Lesson 8 (Page 63)

Resources

- Sticky notes
- Extract (in resource) from *Red Red Shoes*

Lesson 9 (Page 65)

Resources

- A space big enough to perform scenes, with chairs arranged in a semi-circle
- Great cards/question cards (see lesson plan for more details)

Lesson 10 (Page 66)

Resources

- Mini whiteboards (if possible)

CORE PLAYWRITING SCHEME OF WORK
Lesson 1: Opening Scene
PLTS: Creative Thinking
APP: WAF3; RAF3

1 Prepare for and Connect the Learning

Distribute a range of different text types (including poetry, narrative and non-fiction) around the room including short extracts from plays (see resources). Stick them on the walls.

Students work in groups to identify and categorise how they know which ones are plays. What does a script look like on the page? How do you know? What is the purpose of a play? Can it differ? Are plays written to be read or watched or both? Discuss. For more able students reference Stolen Secrets (see resources). Ask students to analyse the beginning of Stolen Secrets and clarify what makes it a drama rather than a poem? How do they know? What about character and location in plays compared to other text types?   **15 min**

2 Agree Learning Objectives

Contextualise SoW.

- **Identify** differences between scripts and other text types
- **Understand** how to begin a scene and engage the audience through conflict between the characters
- **Apply** this new understanding to writing a scene(s)

3 Present New Information Through the Senses

Progress check of learning objectives. Where are we? How do we know?

Reference second learning objective – we're going to understand how to begin a scene and engage the audience through conflict.

Ask the group for different ways of greeting people and write their suggestions on the board. Do not change the spelling of their suggestions and ask for the way they would spell these greetings. They should be different ways of saying hello and get them to think about how they greet different people – e.g. how they greet a friend; how they greet a teacher; how they greet a parent and how they greet a stranger. Give a few examples:

Hello; Hi; Safe; Alright etc. List on board.

Ask the group for different ways of saying 'I don't want to talk to you.' Again ask the group to consider how they say this to a stranger, parent, sibling, friend etc. and give a few examples. List their ideas on the board, e.g.

Sorry, I've got to catch the bus; Leave me alone; Whatever; Laters etc.

Ask the group to choose one of the greetings. This will be the first line of their play and will be the first line for 'A'. Write this on the board so that they can see the layout:

E.g. A: Hi

Now ask the group to choose one from the other list and this will be the first line for 'B'.

E.g. B: Leave me alone.

These will be the first two lines of the scene:

E.g. A: Hi

B: Leave me alone.

Ask pupils for a suggestion for the next line for A:

A: Hi

B: Leave me alone.

A: new line from students

Continue writing scene together. It is important to make it clear to the students that conflict is at the heart of any good drama and it is this conflict that keeps the audience wanting to find out how the characters will react to it. Get students to summarise how they were able to do this and how conflict is demonstrated. What engages the audience? Why? Explain that they will be able to apply what they have learnt later in the lesson when they work in groups to write scenes.   **20 min approx**

The TEEP Learning Cycle

4 Construct

Explain that we are now moving on to consolidate our understanding of beginning a scene and engaging an audience through conflict by analysing part of a scene from a play.

Choose one of the following extracts and students deduce, infer and interpret (RAF3):

What the conflict is or appears to be
What we learn about the characters
Whether the location impacts on what is happening
Different techniques the writer uses

The extracts to choose from (refer to resources) are:
'Make 'n' Mend' from *Stolen Secrets*
Baby Girl
My Face
Listen to Your Parents   **15 min**

5 Apply to Demonstrate your New Understanding

Students revisit scene written as a class. Individually, students add to the original scene based on ideas from the Construct section of the lesson or begin new opening scenes using ideas from the Construct section of the lesson.   **15 min**

6 Review – step back and reflect on your learning

Reflection/Think Time – students write any questions they have on sticky notes and post them to a Question Wall. This is a dedicated space on a wall or on the board where students post questions about their learning.   **5 min**

Extracts

Stolen Secrets by Fin Kennedy (*The Urban Girl's Guide to Camping and other plays*, Nick Hern Books Limited, 2010, pp. 55–6)

Make 'n' Mend

MOTHER.	I want that pile finished by the time we close. Understand?
DAUGHTER.	Yes, Mum.
NARRATORS.	But only a hundred yards away

The delights of Brick Lane
Roasting meat
Shisha pipes
The tinkle of laughter
And the sweet scent of freedom
Waft across the summer air
And tug at the Daughter's heart.

DAUGTHER.	Mum?
MOTHER.	What?
DAUGHTER.	If I finish early –
MOTHER.	You won't.
DAUGHTER.	But if I do –
MOTHER.	The answer's no. Get on with your work.
NARRATORS.	Of course, what the daughter really wants to say is:
DAUGHTER.	You know what my greatest fear is? Turning into a lonely, bitter, ugly old woman. Just. Like. YOU!
NARRATORS:	The ball of longing inside her

Wants to grab her mother and shout:

DAUGHTER:	I am not your prisoner! Not your slave!

Baby Girl by Roy Williams (NT Connections 2007 New Plays for Young People, Faber and Faber Limited, 2007, p. 7)

APRIL

Sam enters, hovering, singing along to 'Hung UP' by Madonna which is coming from the radio. Kelle, her daughter, enters, wearing an extremely short skirt. Sam turns the radio off.

Kelle	Yeah, what?
Sam	I don't think so, somehow.
Kelle	Oh Mum!
Sam	No, no, no.
Kelle	What?
Sam	Don't you 'Mum' me.
Kelle	Oh sorry, Sam!
Sam	Oy!
Kelle	Well, which one is it, Mum or Sam?
Sam	Kelle?
Kelle	What?
Sam	I'm not playing.
Kelle	At what, Sam...I mean Mum?
Sam	You winding me up.

Kelle sighs
I know all of the tricks, yeah. I did it with your gran.

Kelle Is it?
Sam Yes it is. And do you know what? I was better.
Kelle Do I look like I'm playing any tricks?
Sam Yes you are.
Kelle All I want to do is wear my skirt.
Sam No way.
Kelle Ain't that short.
Sam You sure?!

My Face by Nigel Williams (New Connections 2008 Plays for Young People, Faber and Faber Limited, 2008, p. 319)

Mark Susie and Lou have known each other for ever. Susie bosses Lou around something shocking. But then – she bosses everyone around. I think Lou put a picture of a gorilla up on My Face because she is so amazingly hot that she would be stalked unmercifully if her real picture got out there.

Lou   Hi Susie!
Susie Hi Lou!
Lou   How are you, Susie?
Susie I'm good, Lou. How are you?
Lou   I'm good.

She takes off the gorilla costume and addresses the audience.

I'm not actually good. I'm really really depressed. Because I'm fat.

As she takes off the suit we see she is in fact amazingly thin.

I hate how I look. Which is why I put the gorilla picture up on My Face.

She holds out the mask in front of her.

That is so much better-looking than me.

Listen to Your Parents by Benjamin Zephaniah (*Theatre Centre plays for young people Vol. 1*, Aurora Metro Publications Ltd, reprinted 2008, pp. 24–6)

Note:

The play is set in and around the home of the Campbells, a Black British family living in Birmingham. The Campbell family consists of Mark and his Mom and Dad – his sister Angela and baby Carlton need not appear.

1. **MONDAY**

   Mark is sitting on his bed looking in his bag.

   Wali addresses the audience from a platform/pulpit.

   WALI On the first day God created the heavens and the Earth. Then he created flowers and trees, and humans beings and living stuff that creep upon the surface of the Earth. And he looked down upon the Earth and he saw that it was good. Then for some strange reason he created school. And Mark Campbell attended one such school in the great land known as Birmingham. And it was there that Mark Campbell created a great opportunity for himself, and he went for it.

   They both break into football terrace style chants.

   BOTH Villa *(clap, clap, clap)* Villa *(clap, clap, clap)* Villa *(clap, clap, clap)*

   Mark addresses the audience.

   MARK Yes this is it, I can't wait. I could be playing for Aston Villa. Me, Aston Villa, brilliant innit? And here it is, look at this, *(Takes shirt out of bag)* – me Aston Villa shirt. I wanted the whole kit but Mom said she couldn't afford it, but the shirt's OK, no it's more than OK, it's wicked guy. I wasn't even doing anything special, just playing around on the pitch after school and I could see this bloke standing there with Mr. Collins the P.E. teacher. At first I thought he was a parent or something. Then when we finished playing Mr Collins called me over and I thought, O, O, I'm in trouble again, but I wasn't.

The bloke said, 'I've heard a lot about you Mark. What are you doing next Saturday afternoon?' So I said, 'Playing football,' and he said, 'Do you want to go to Villa Park and play some football?' And I said, 'What actually *in* Villa Park?' And he said, 'Yes lad, we're having trials, we're looking for some players for the junior team and you look pretty good to me. And then I started to tell him that I wasn't even playing my best today and that I usually score about three goals in every game, and that I play even better on a full-size pitch, but he said I should save all me energy for Saturday. *(Mark chants)* Villa, Villa, Villa.

Music.

Mark picks up his book and begins to read.

MARK Red ripe Mangoes on Lozell's Road

Ackees on Heatfield,

And Callaloo for all on Witton Road,

Jamaica must be here somewhere.

There's Reggae in the morning

Reggae at noon

And Reggae is played on Soho Road at night

For grown ups and foxes alike.

Jamaica must be here somewhere.

Coconuts and cashew nuts cook themselves,

And the aunties and the uncles

Walk like they have springs in their feet

And drums on their minds,

Is this Jamaica?

Jamaica must be here somewhere,

I can taste it,

I can smell it,

Everybody is talking about it,

There are Jamaican newspapers in the corner shops

And Jamaican curls in my hair,

You can't fool me.

Jamaica must be here somewhere.

Pause.

I got two of these books, both actually the same, one for me and one for me Mom. I wrote the poems meself and sellotaped them together. Look, see what it says there? Published by Mark Anthony Campbell – Limited. And there's the title, it's called *'Life'.*

This scene was written by a Year 8 student working at level 3 of the National Curriculum for English.

[also relevant to Objectives and obstacles – Lesson 8]

Cheesy Feet Man and the Disaster by Tyran Jones, Year 8

Cheesy Feet Man is in an aftershave company.
Cheesy Feet Man goes into the aftershave company running after a burglar. When he comes back his feet smell like roses.

CFM:	OMG AHHHHHHHHHHHH MY feet!!!!!!!!!!
Old Man:	Mmmmmmmmm what is that smell? It smells like my garden.

Cheesy Feet Man starts to cry. Then he sees a skunk run by.

CFM:	Come here little skunk.
Old Man:	What do you want that skunk for?
CFM:	Never you mind.

Cheesy Feet Man turns red in the face and starts to run after the skunk and bumps into the President of the USA.

President:	Do you want a hamburger?
CFM:	Has it got cheese on it?
President:	Course it has.
CFM:	I'll take one.

Meanwhile the skunk is running round like a headless chicken and bumps into a Policeman.

Policeman:	Somebody get that skunk off my feet.
CFM:	Keep him there I WANT THAT SKUNK.
	(Choking on his hamburger)
Policeman:	Come here you smelly vermin.

He grabs the skunk and tries to handcuff him but instead he handcuffs himself.

Policeman:	Damn you I'm going to get you skunk.
Skunk:	Not if I get you first mahahahahahahahaha.

The skunk sprays all over the Policeman's feet.

CFM:	Come over here to me skunk. (smirks)
Skunk:	Why? *(Reluctantly)* What do you want me for? I smell nice just like your feet.
CFM:	I know but if you do spray me my feet will smell extra nice.
Policeman:	Are you mad?
Skunk:	OK, I will do it for a fee.
CFM:	What do you want then?
Skunk:	Ten hamburgers fresh from the USA.
CFM:	*(Shouting)* President come here.
President:	*(Walking over to CFM)* What do you want?
CFM:	Hamburgers. Ten of them.
President:	I only have eight.

CORE PLAYWRITING SCHEME OF WORK
Lesson 2: Stories are Everywhere
PLTS: Creative Thinking; Teamwork;
Self-Management
APP: S&L AF1

1 Prepare for and Connect the Learning

On desks or stuck on walls are pre-prepared photographs/pictures and/or current news stories and pictures. Ensure they are a varied mix and show different images from around the world and different cultures, situations, contexts etc. Students write down any questions that the photos prompt on sticky notes and stick them to the photographs or write in the space around the photos. You could prompt the students by asking them to think about who the people are in the photos and what are they doing.

5 min

2 Agree Learning Objectives
- **Identify** ideas for our plays using different stimuli
- **Synthesise** our partner's ideas and **explain** them to the rest of the group

3 Present New Information Through the Senses

Teacher then instructs students to get up out of their seats and walk around, looking carefully at all the pictures and all the questions and comments.

10 minutes silent Thinking Time – students are then given the time to write any ideas down in their books/journals that the photos have prompted. They should be able to get up out of their seats and look at the photos again at any time during this 10-minute Thinking Time.

Teacher explains how music is very evocative and can be an excellent stimulus to the writing process. Teacher plays pre-selected piece of music (anything that is evocative, preferably without lyrics) and students close their eyes and listen to the music. Alternatively, you could have a carousel of different 'music stations' around the room (mp3 players; computers) where students listen to a number of different tracks. Students write in their book/journal what the music makes them think of – any words, phrases or images.

Discuss ideas as a whole group. Remind students there are no right or wrong answers; it's all about their own ideas.

NB – if you would like to read about further writing strategies and exercises to use with your students, please see Noël Greig's book *Playwriting: A Practical Guide* (reading list)

20 min

6 Review – step back and reflect on your learning

Students come up to the front to present their mini introductions to their partner and bring their 'prop' to the front (their partner).

20 min

5 Apply to Demonstrate your New Understanding

Students work in pairs finding out five key things about their partner's play ideas. They then write a short introduction to their partner beginning with something like, 'Esteemed colleagues, I'd now like to welcome our after-dinner speaker . . .' Share level descriptors for S&L AF1 (talking to others) so pupils can identify their target level (see bibliography).

Students spend no longer than 10 minutes writing their mini introduction speeches.

Speeches need only be 2–3 minutes long.

15 min

The TEEP Learning Cycle

4 Construct

Students now reflect on their ideas and choose an idea for their story. It could be taken from any of the ideas from last lesson or from today. It could be taken from any of the ideas that your partners' ideas and present them to the class.

Students write one paragraph about what their play is about and five key events that could happen in the play.

Explain to the group that we are now going to work in pairs to synthesise (pull together) our partners' ideas and present them to the class.
So it means we are going to have to use our listening skills to listen to our partners very carefully, and also our skills of self-management to be organised and work to time.
Explain that they are going to introduce their partner to the rest of the group as a famed playwright who will be an after-dinner speaker. Their task is to find out five fascinating facts about their partner's play and turn it into an introduction to their partner for the rest of the group, pretending their partner is a famed, award-winning playwright. You might want to show the group a clip of a similar introduction to after-dinner speakers etc. (see YouTube for ideas).

5 min

Additionally, students could research some of the playwrights on the reading list for further ideas and inspiration: Fin Kennedy, Roy Williams and Benjamin Zephaniah are all award-winning playwrights.

CORE PLAYWRITING SCHEME OF WORK

Lesson 3: Character

PLTS: Creative Thinking; Reflective Learning

APP: RAF2; RAF3

---

1 Prepare for and Connect the Learning

Sticky notes are given to everyone in the group – one each. Write down something you want (this can be anonymous). The want must be something that would change things for you if you had it, and also something that you don't mind sharing with the group, e.g. if I had my own bedroom I could write a bestselling book as I wouldn't be distracted by my little brother. I could then buy my family a bigger house with all the money. Try to pre-empt any silly suggestions!

Everyone stick their sticky note up on the wall around the room.

5 min

---

2 Agree Learning Objectives

- **Identify** quotations from a play to back up what you think about the characters
- **Infer** what the characters' wants are in an extract from the play
- **Create** our own character histories considering what our characters want

---

3 Present New Information Through the Senses

Students move around the room reading everyone's wants. In pairs, discuss the following questions:

What things might you have wanted to know more about?

How are people to achieve this?

What stands in the way?

Does it conceal something else?

Why is that want so important?

Share some of the ideas as a class.

10 min

---

4 Construct

Teacher links this activity to the journey of a character in a play. For characters to be believable and for plays to drive forward, the character(s) in the play need a WANT (an objective). All characters in a play have an over-arching want – a super-objective. All the smaller 'wants' (objectives) in each scene build towards this big want. Think of something a character might do in a scene to get something they want – e.g. money, true love, peace of mind etc. Discuss ideas as a class.

Read one (or more if you have time) of the following extracts (ref reading list):

School Journey to the Centre of the Earth

'Not a Girl' from *Stolen Secrets*

15 min

The TEEP Learning Cycle

---

5 Apply to Demonstrate your New Understanding

As a whole group, focus on information retrieval and using quotations (RAF2). Focus on one character from one of the extracts you have read as a class. Draw a Role on the Wall on the board (either an outline of a person or the outline of a head). The class may have done this before in English or drama. Explain to them that the inside represents how the character is feeling and the outside of the figure/head represents what other people think of that character. Group suggest ideas about how character is feeling. Write the suggestion in the figure/head on the board (or get a volunteer to). Now, crucially, ask the group to find a quotation to back that up. Students write that under the suggested adjective. Do the same with what other people think about the character but on the outside of the figure/head. Having modelled two or three ideas the class should be able to do it themselves in their books and could move on to inferring and deducing information about another character from the extract.

Develop further. What can we infer or deduce about this character (or other characters) from what they say or do?

Students add ideas to the character ideas in their books.

20–25 min

---

6 Review – step back and reflect on your learning

Students now spend some time researching publicly-viewable Facebook status updates and Tweets (this may need to be a homework activity, depending on your access to social networking sites in school), or alternatively share some status updates/Tweets that you have already researched for them. Students share some of the status updates and Tweets they have found or ones provided. Question class: what sort of character could this be? What can we infer from this status update/Tweet about this person? Use them as a starting point for generating ideas about characters. They could even become the first line of the students' plays, e.g. 'Some heifer has got my man.'; 'I say my dad's unhelpful … but he still puts credit on my phone for me.' How does this person speak? What do we learn about them from the way they speak? This also introduces some of the ideas about character and speech that the students will explore next lesson.

Thinking Time. Refocus group to begin to think about their own characters in their own plays. What are their characters' wants? How will they speak? Can you use any of these ideas from social media as a starting point for your play?

15 min

Extracts

School Journey to the Centre of the Earth by Daisy Campbell, with Ken Campbell (*Shell Connections 2006 New Plays for Young People*, Faber and Faber Limited, pp. 468–70)

Stacey (*to James*) I don't think Miracle's got a TV.

Chrissy *and* **Bee** What?

Stacey All that rubbish about *War of the Worlds*. I reckon she hasn't got one.

Chrissy Yeah, and she reckoned the reason Alfie was vexed was because Kat was doing sex with someone!

Stacey *and* **Bee** (*amazed*) No!

Bee (*leaning in to the conversation*) When I went to her house she said it was at the mender's.

Stacey How long ago was that?

Bee About three months ago.

James She ain't got a TV? Oy, Rab, Get this, Miracle ain't got a telly!

Rab Rah! Miracle! Are you a tramp or what? (*in front of the whole coach*) Ain't you got a telly?

Everyone laughs

Miracle What?

James You ain't got a telly!

Miracle Of course I do.

James Oo yeah.

Miracle I do.

Rab Alright then. How does the Muller advert go then?

Miracle Isn't that the one when – there's the mum at the breakfast –

Everyone NO! Five – six – seven – eight.

Everyone Got my hair, got my head, got my brains, got my ears, got my eyes, got my nose, got my mouth, got my smile. Got my tongue, got my chin, got my bum, got my boobs, got my heart, got my soul, got my liver, got my sex. I got my freedom, freedom. I got life.

Rab Lead a Muller Life!

Everyone T-E-L-L-Y, T-E-L-L-Y, T-E-L-L-Y. You ain't got a telly!

The chant gets faster and faster and more and more in Miracle's face. All repeat until Miracle breaks down.

Miracle (*through terrible sobs*) You don't know what it's like. My mum won't let me have one. She says it rots your brain. She makes me do stuff in the garden and draw and read and play the saxophone instead. She's so horrible. She's like a witch. I hate her so much.

Tricia Miracle, don't worry. It's not that bad. (*Pause, then declares loudly.*) I haven't got one either.

Miracle Really?

James (*to Tricia*) Urggh, you filthy tramp. Get back in your cardboard box.

Everyone starts teasing Tricia.

Jenelle Oh my God! Shut up! Can anyone else hear that ticking?

The paranoia builds up as they search for the source of the ticking, finally traced to – Rab.

Rab Booom!

Screams

Jenelle That is not even funny, Rab. Now that we know Miss Sheehankov is a terrorist you shouldn't make jokes like that –

Sam Jenelle, don't worry. They need us to be alive – so they can watch us, right, Trish?

Tom Brainwash us more like.

Rab (*popping up*) Shut up, Tom. Loser!

Tricia No, Rab. He's right. I didn't want to say this. But the experiment isn't to watch us. The experiment is to brainwash us. To turn us into Nasties.

Janelle Why?

Tricia So that we will end up like Miss Sheehankov. Pretending to be a nice teacher what supports Arsenal so that we can capture more kids to brainwash. It's a vikkious cycle.

Miracle What are we gonna do, Trish?

Tricia We'll make a break for it when we're down there and hide out in this cave I know about the terrorists don't know and keep guard –

Janelle Will we have someone on guard all night for the Nasties?

Tricia Er – yeah.

Janelle Do I have to do it, Tricia? I don't think girls should have to do it.

Tricia No, sorry. Everyone has to do it.

James (*popping up*) I'll do it. It'll be like *Tomb Raider*.

Mimes shooting up Nasties with deadly precision.

Mega-death.

Mimes gore-and-blood splatterfest.

Jenelle Can I be partners with you, James? I think I'll feel safest with you.

James (*suddenly shy and coy*) Yeah, alright. If you like.

Sonny Jenelle? Don't you want to be partners with me?

***Stolen Secrets* by Fin Kennedy (*The Urban Girl's Guide to Camping and other plays*, Nick Hern Books Limited, 2010, pp. 68–9)**

Not a Girl

NARRATORS. There's this girl lives down Limehouse way

Near where the canal meets Bartlett Park

Nasima

Nice enough

So long as you stay on her good side

This girl can handle herself, innit.

NASIMA. What you saying?

NARRATORS. Nuttin

Chill, man

There's boys scared of this chick, narmsayin.

NASIMSA. What you chattin?

NARRATORS. Allow it, man.

She's nineteen, yeah

So a year out of college

But unemployed the whole time

But not cos she ain't clever or nuttin

No way, this girl is smart

Wanted to go university

But to study Engineering

And that's where it all fell apart.

MUM. Why can't you study teaching or nursing like a normal girl?

NASIMA. I am normal. I just wanna do engineering, innit.

DAD. No daughter of mine will be doing this.

NASIMA. Why not?

DAD. I will not pay for such a perversion!

NASIMA. Why not?

MUM. Are you a boy or a girl?

NASIMA. Girl, I spose.

DAD. Well start acting like it then!

NARRATORS. Nasima's always been a tomboy, yeah

Everyone always says it

And she feels it herself.

CORE PLAYWRITING SCHEME OF WORK
Lesson 4: Character and speech
PLTS: Creative Thinking; Reflective Learning
APP: RAF7; RAF5

1 Prepare for and Connect the Learning

Image on interactive whiteboard of a suitcase or bag. Or, ideally, have a suitcase or large bag at the front. Students write questions in their books/journals that they have about the suitcase, e.g. what's in it, who does it belong to etc. Reveal next image on board as a PowerPoint or take an object out of the suitcase. Explain it's an object belonging to a character – a character who owns the suitcase. In pairs, students discuss what this might tell them about the character who owns the suitcase.

Do this again with two or three more objects. Give students Thinking Time to discuss in their groups/pairs. Whole-class discussion. **10 min**

Write ideas on flipchart.

2 Agree Learning Objectives

- **Create** our own character histories
- **Analyse** speech patterns and **apply** these ideas to our own characters

3 Present New Information Through the Senses

Explain that the activity we have just worked through has enabled us to build up a picture of the person, or character, that owns the suitcase. We have started to build our characters and their wants. Think of your main character based on your ideas so far, and draw objects that he/she would carry in their suitcase and write next to them what it reveals about them and where and how their character acquired these objects. Students begin to build up the stories and events of their characters' journeys.

Students complete character histories (see resources). **15 min**

The TEEP Learning Cycle

4 Construct

One of the questions on your character history sheet was asking you to think about the way your main character speaks – his or her idiolect that is unique to them. Link this to the work they have done on characters and social media – Facebook status updates and Tweets – and the way people speak and what we learn about them and can infer. Introduce students to a range of extracts from different plays (see suggested extracts below).

Each group could be given an extract or alternatively the extracts could be enlarged and stuck on walls around the room and pupils move around the space reading and analysing them. For each extract, ask the students to identify and analyse the different speech patterns of the characters. How do the characters speak? Why? Does the social, cultural or historical context of the play or social or cultural backgrounds of the characters affect this? Does the location of the play affect this? Do other characters affect this? What do we learn about the characters from the way they speak? What facts? What presumptions? What do we find out about their relationships? What's going on in their homes? What's going on in their towns? Analysing the extracts, focus on the teaching of RAF7 (relate texts to their social, cultural and historical traditions) and RAF5 (explain and comment on writer's use of language, including grammatical and literary features at word and sentence level). You can use the work the students produce here to assess against these AFs.

Suggested extracts:

Listen to Your Parents
Fugee
The Mother Ship

20–25 min

5 Apply to Demonstrate your New Understanding

Reference second learning objective. Explain how we have analysed speech patterns and also thought about our main character's life history in detail, including how they speak. Students now revisit the first scene they were working on. They will need to reference their ideas from earlier lessons for ideas. Students make amendments and changes based on their characters' idiolects.

15 min

6 Review – step back and reflect on your learning

Hand out sticky notes. As students leave, they write down one word or phrase that typifies the way their main character speaks; a word or phrase that their main character might use all the time. Stick on board as they leave the room.

5 min

Extracts

Listen to Your Parents by Benjamin Zephaniah (*Theatre Centre Plays for Young People Vol. 1*, Aurora Metro Publications Ltd, reprinted 2008, pp. 31–2)

DAD *(still preaching)* But what is going wrong? We need to analyse the situation and consider what is to be done. We need to ask ourselves, what is it that we need to do, to save ourselves from the brimstone and the fire. Well, my people, the answer is simple, praise the Lord. The truth is that this is not a complex or a difficult thing. We must do two things, Hallelujah. We must let the world know that Christ is not history, Christ is living, Christ is now, and we must put back the Lord Jesus Christ into our lives, we must bring Jesus right into the culture of society. Christ must be the inspiration for all our politicians, Christ must be the inspiration for all of our teachers, he will lead us out of the darkness, he will lead us into the light, Christ himself must lead the way. Thank God.

Crowd response.

DAD Praise Jesus. And secondly we must rebuild the family – the family is the rock that holds up society. If you don't have discipline in the family, how can we have discipline in the schools? If you don't have discipline in the family, how can you have discipline in the factories? How in the name of God, can we have discipline on the streets, if there is no discipline in the family? God is the father, God is the son, God created families for us because families work best. Let me hear you praise the Lord.

CROWD Praise the Lord.

DAD Let me hear you say, Hallelujah.

CROWD Hallelujah!

Light on Mark.

MARK *(turning to audience)* I reckon Jesus spoke soft and quietly like. I reckon he had manners, you know what I mean? He would say great wise things that would make people be 'Cool', bet he would drop phat lyrics guy, I don't think he'd be shouting his mouth off like a mad man.

Fugee by Abi Morgan (*New Shell Connections 2008 Plays for Young People*, Faber and Faber Limited, 2008, pp. 148–51)

Ara They show videos on Friday. Except when they break down. They always break. Then there's ping pong. Ping Pong?

(To audience.) We don't speak the same language. This is a refuge. It's where they bring all the fugees. All the fugees who have got here, here into this country, your United Kingdom, on their own or even with someone and maybe they are now on their own.

Unaccompanied minors. That's him. That's me. I came in a lorry. *(Beat.)* To stay here you have to be under sixteen.

Silence.

What you got?

Kojo Huh?

Ara Behind your –

Kojo hesitates, holds out a photo. Ara takes it, smiling on seeing –

That your – ?

Kojo's Brother enters, a football under his arm.

Smiling, as if posing for a photograph.

Kojo Brother.

Kojo's Father enters, joining Kojo's Brother, a look of surprise, hand over his eyes, as if squinting in the sun.

Ara Abba.

Kojo Papa.

Ara You've got his ears. *(Gesturing)* Ears.

Kojo No.

Ara Yeah.

Kojo laughs. Ara laughs. Kojo points to the photo.

Ara She's pretty.

Kojo's Mother enters, face freezing mid-laughter, the photo taken.

Kojo nods.

Kojo holds out his hand. Ara hands him back the photograph. Kojo's family exits.

Ara Don't put it on the wall. The other kids...

Kojo Huh?

Ara Keep it in your pocket...

Pocket. The other kids nick photos.

The Mothership by Douglas Maxwell (Oberon Books Limited, 2008, pp. 20–1)

Some of that goddamn bedroom music.

It's KEVIN's room and he is raging. He paces like a lawyer in a film. He doesn't look like a lawyer though. He's still wearing his uniform from work. A bright yellow T-Shirt with 'LIFEGUARD' printed on it. Come to think of it, he doesn't look much like a lifeguard either.

ELIOT is lying back on the bed reading a crumpled letter.

KEVIN So he come slimping into the Sunken Tsunami Zone, his trucking toad face all, like, toading out all over the joint. I was like, 'What does this daft bar steward want now?' So he starts screaming all like 'I know it was you McCloy'. And I was like 'Prove it'. So he turns round and says 'I don't need to prove it. I know it was you that wrote the letter, so pack your flipflops and hit the bricks.' 'No way,' I goes, 'this is unfair dismissal. I've been a lifeguard at this pool since before I could swim. You chuck me out and I'm going to tribunal. Where's your proof?' He says 'No proof necessary. I can tell you wrote it from the language.'

ELIOT *(Reading.)* 'Dear Dicks, Any dick that goes to this meeting is a dick.' And it's signed, 'Mr and Mrs Piss'.

KEVIN So I says 'Well that's where you're wrong Toadteeth, cos I don't swear'.

ELIOT Except that you do.

KEVIN Not anymore.

ELIOT Yeah right.

KEVIN Nope. I've changed it.

ELIOT What do you mean?

KEVIN I've changed it. I was up all night reprogramming my linguistic hard-drive. He'll never trip me up. I'll show him. Little toad faced motherfunster. I'll never swear again.

ELIOT Oh so that's why you're talking funny.

Character History Sheet

• Where was your character born?	
• When were they born?	
• Who were their parents or adult carers?	
• What sort of family/home life did they have?	
• What sort of education did they have?	
• What was a good early experience they had?	
• What was a bad early experience they had?	

• Who or what made them what they are?	
• What does your character need or want right now?	
• What words or phrases does your character use frequently? The technical term for this is a person's (or character's) **idiolect** – language that is unique to them.	
• What secret does your character have?	

CORE PLAYWRITING SCHEME OF WORK
Lesson 5: Opening Moment/Scene
PLTS: Creative Thinking; Reflective Learning
APP: WAF3

1 **Prepare for and Connect the Learning**

Big Question on board as students enter:

Think about where your play begins. What is happening in your character's life at that point in time?

Thinking Time.

5 min

2 **Agree Learning Objectives**

- **Analyse** an opening scene to a play and **explain** what makes it effective
- **Apply** these ideas to the opening scene for our own plays

3 **Present New Information Through the Senses**

Reference first learning objective and introduce extract – explain that it is taken from a play called *The Miracle* (see resources). What is a miracle? What can we infer from the title of the play? What might it be about? Read extract from *The Miracle*. Check understanding of extract. Question group. Refer to first learning objective. What made the opening of the scene effective? Think, Pair, Share. Students think individually for 2 minutes or so, then pair up with a partner to discuss, then share ideas with the whole class. List on flipchart or board. Focus on WAF3 here and how the structuring of this scene is effective.

E.g.
Tensions between characters
A hint of things to come
A sense of the characters' wants etc.
Incongruity
Location

20 min

The TEEP Learning Cycle

4 **Construct**

Explain that now we have identified what makes an effective play opening, we are going to have a go at refining openings of our own plays.
Explain the following to the students (write on the board or give as a handout if need be):
Look back at the work you've done on your characters and the scene that you started writing a few lessons ago.
Choose a moment in the life of your character with which to open the play.
Include at least two characters.
Go for something low-key, but with hints and suggestions of conflicts and tensions beneath the surface.
Bring in something to mark it as different from all the other days.
Try for a scene of some length – at least two pages in your writing journals.
Don't worry if it doesn't complete itself, focus on getting the characters talking.

10 min max.

6 **Review – step back and reflect on your learning**

Individuals read out some opening scenes.
Other students reflect and feed back on characters, location, tension and conflict, wants etc.

15 min

5 **Apply to Demonstrate your New Understanding**

Students spend the next 20 minutes writing their opening scene, using the guidance on the board and ideas from earlier in the lesson.

As a starting point, get them to emulate the stage directions used in *The Miracle*, but adapt it to their own setting. See examples from year 8 students at Shenley Academy working at level 2 and 3 for English (see resources).

20 min

Extracts

The Miracle by Lin Coghlan (*Shell Connections 2006 New Plays for Young People*, Faber and Faber Limited, 2006, p. 231)

A town, somewhere in the British Isles. Night.

The population of the town stand looking across the rooftops, as if remembering.

The rain cascades onto pavements, shop fronts and guttering.

Ron and Zelda stand amongst the throng. Ron has a pineapple in her hand.

Zelda No one believed us, said we was making it all up, But we never. In't that right, Ron?

Ron Yeah.

Zelda We never. It all happened just like we said, that weird week.

Ron Freak, they said it was.

Zelda That storm.

Ron Rain come down, what was it like, Zel?

Zelda Ain't never seen nothing like it. Wasn't long after that we had the miracle.

Ron Come up through me floor, right next to the bunk beds.

Billy You hear that, Mum? I heard something – next door.

Ron Heard it next door, they did.

Zelda Billy Hammond heard it when he was in the bath, said he heard voices, came up through the plug hole.

Ron But he was having us on.

Zelda I mean, why would Billy Hammond get a miracle up his plug hole?

Ron And you don't get two miracles in one night, do you?

Opening scenes by Year 8 students. These students were working at level 2 or level 3 of the National Curriculum for English.

Theme Park by Jonathan McCann, Year 8

A theme park, somewhere in the British Isles

11.00 am

Bernie is stuck on the highest point of Apocalypse. The ride has stopped and is stuck.

Bernie: (shouting very loudly) Help!!!!

Bernie closes his eyes because he is so scared.

Man (shouting): I'll get you down!!!!

The bars open at the top. Bernie is hanging on by his fingertips.

Claire: Hang on Dad I am coming to get you down.

She puts on her costume and climbs up the side of the ride.

Aliens from Mars **by Eloise Millership, Year 8**

A planet called Mars somewhere in space. It is never daytime. Liam is standing looking far out into space with his friend Alany, talking. Suddenly Liam starts to feel dizzy and in a flash Liam grows spots. Alany runs away and takes the space boat back down to Earth.

Liam: What's happening? *(Liam starts to appear yellow spots)*

Alany: Go away. Aaaaaaaaaaaaa.

Liam: Wait up. I won't bite.

Alany: I don't care. Go away.

Liam: Where are you?

Liam loses track of Alany and all of a sudden the planet shakes and Liam sees Alany in the space boat.

Liam: COME BACK.

Alany: No you spotty freak.

Liam: Don't go. *(Liam cries and walks to the end of the planet and Liam waves goodbye as Alany goes down to Earth.)*

Alany: Why did he change to spots? What if I caught it?

Alany starts to cry as she leaves the planet.

Football Match by Ryan Wakelam and Reece Barnes, Year 8

Agent Reece: Ryan has hurt his leg it is very serious.

A football stadium at lunchtime. The fans in the stadium stand looking across the pitch. They are looking at Ryan to see if he is injured. Ryan is sprawled on the pitch, the blood is dribbling from his leg.

Ryan: Ow!!

Ryan rocks on the ground and gripping his leg then the ref blows whistle and sends other people off.

Terry: What the hell man?

Swears at the ref so Terry gets banned for a month. He walks off crying.

Then Ryan is crying and he has a penalty.

Ryan: Yes.

Crowd going wild.

On the roof of the stadium the hit man is trying to shoot Ryan because he wants him to pay back his money.

The ref blows the whistle for half time.

CORE PLAYWRITING SCHEME OF WORK

Lesson 6: Location and Environment
PLTS: Creative Thinking; Reflective Learning
APP: WAF1

1 Prepare for and Connect the Learning

Big Question on board as students enter:

What's the difference between location and environment?
Think on your own, pair your ideas with a partner, share with the rest of the group.

Discuss.

5 min

2 Agree Learning Objectives

- **Explain** how the location and environment affects our characters
- **Analyse** how location affects characters in a different extract
- **Create** a scene in a specific location

3 Present New Information Through the Senses

Around the room have various pictures and photos of different locations – e.g. train station, library, hospital ward, car park, shopping centre, airport, park, school corridor, the moon etc. Students walk around the room 'reading' the pictures/photos etc. For each location they need to explain how it might affect their main character and why. How might their main character react or behave in that location? Write on sticky note and attach to picture.

10 min

The TEEP Learning Cycle

4 Construct

Ref second learning objective. Students imagine their main character is trapped at the top of a large building (e.g. a tower block), looking down at the world carrying on beneath them. Students consider how location and environment become characters too and make people behave in certain ways – main character's world inside; other characters outside. More able pupils should be encouraged to explore this idea in further depth.

Ask students to imagine they are writing as their main character, in role. Students continue to explore their main character, trapped at the top of a tower block or another large building. What do they see? How do they feel? Students write a monologue in role. Alternatively, using the same location this could be adapted (depending on the class) from a monologue to:

Main character's Facebook status updates
Main character's series of Tweets over a time period
Main character's text messages to different characters in the play
NB – these ideas or the monologue can be incorporated into the students' plays if they so wish, or can be used as a stand-alone exercise to explore character and location.

25–30 min

5 Apply to Demonstrate your New Understanding

Students choose a location from the ideas on the walls or think of their own.
Students write the next scene for their play in a specific location. They must think about how their character would react and behave in that specific location. How might it affect how they speak or behave?

20 min

6 Review – step back and reflect on your learning

Thinking Time: students reflect on the writing they have created so far today and what further ideas they have about their plays.

5 min

CORE PLAYWRITING SCHEME OF WORK
Lesson 7: Structure and timeframe
PLTS: Creative Thinking; Reflective Learning
APP: WAF1; WAF3

1 Prepare for and Connect the Learning

Welcome. Play 'washing line' strung up in room as students enter. Different pieces of clothing on washing line (these don't have to be real clothes but could be different-sized pieces of paper/card if you prefer. Clothes work well though!). Question class: how does this washing line represent a play?

Tease out from the group how the different pieces of clothing represent different-sized scenes and that each scene is a unit of action along the way to the end of the play.

10 min

2 Agree Learning Objectives

- **Identify** the different units of action in our plays and the timeframe of our plays
- **Create** a further three scenes for our plays, using our timeframes

10 min

3 Present New Information Through the Senses

Students consider their own play 'washing lines'. Refer back to the second lesson and the five key events that they decided would happen in their play. In their books/journals, pupils draw a washing line (or they could create literal washing lines!) and add the different-sized scenes, deciding whether they are small, medium or large units of action and outlining how the character(s) is/are changed by the end of each scene.

15 min

The TEEP Learning Cycle

4 Construct

Ask the students to consider how their plays will be structured and how scenes will be sequenced and why (reference WAF3). The washing line follows a linear, sequential model but it doesn't have to be like that. Plays can jump forwards and backwards in time, too. Playwrights also use dramatic devices to propel the action forward and build tension.

Provide the following examples of plays for students to read in class (in additional lessons) or at home to give them ideas about dramatic structure and dramatic devices:

The chorus as a character in itself, helping to push the story forward – *Stolen Secrets; Red Red Shoes*
The use of monologues to explore multiple realities and worlds within a play, but still active and in the present, not reflective – *My Face; Listen to Your Parents; The Urban Girl's Guide to Camping*
Symbolic objects – *Red Red Shoes; 'Make 'n' Mend' (Stolen Secrets); The Miracle; Fugee; The Urban Girl's Guide to Camping*
Repetition of scenes and repeated linguistic riffs – *Liar; My Face*
Characters 'creating' the world of the play – *School Journey to the Centre of the Earth*
In *School Journey to the Centre of the Earth* the characters physicalise different events that they think might happen – e.g. the rollercoaster.

You could spend some time this lesson (or in an additional lesson) exploring one or more of these elements of dramatic structure or dramatic devices, depending on the ability of the group. It's important to consider how structure is intrinsically linked to the characters' journey, and any decisions on structure (and first, timeframe) must be about pushing the story forward. So, in effect, the structure becomes another character. Encourage students to look at their starting point and where they want the character to end up; they should look at the events that change the character.

20 min – but you may want to spend another lesson exploring some of these ideas

5 Apply to Demonstrate your New Understanding

Students now write any three scenes of their play, using their play 'washing line' to help. The scenes don't have to be linear; they can be from any point in the play and can introduce new characters.

20 min

6 Review – step back and reflect on your learning

Explain to the group that the lesson after next will be a workshop lesson where we workshop our plays with actors to see what improvements we could make.

Students instructed to have play scripts typed out (it doesn't matter if they're not finished) and ready to hand in for copying so the actors have enough copies.

5 min

Extract

The Urban Girl's Guide to Camping by Fin Kennedy (*The Urban Girl's Guide to Camping and other plays*, **Nick Hern Books Limited, 2010, pp. 142–4**)

RAJNA. Hair Straighteners?

THAMANNA. Yeah, why not? You can all borrow em.

RAJNA. And where are you gonna plug those in?

THAMANNA *holds up a bulky solar-powered charger.*

THAMANNA. Sola-powered charger.

PARVIN. You think of everything.

RAJNA. Where did you get that?

THAMANNA. My brother.

PARVIN. Your brother thinks of everything.

SABINA (*to audience*). So I'm not saying these people are real

They're not

I've just made them up

This one here –

She goes over to THAMANNA.

Let's call her Thamanna

Yeah

I like that name

I've never met Thamanna

But I may as well have

Cos she's like a lot of people I know

A contradiction

A beautician by day

On her days off she works for the police as one of those Pretend Officers.

THAMANNA. They ain't pretend!

SABINA. What are they then?

THAMANNA. They're real.

SABINA. PCSOs?

THAMANNA. Yeah.

SABINA. My brother says it stands for Pretend Coppers Sod Off.

THAMANNA. Yeah, well, Abdul hardly spends his time on the right side of the law, does he?

Small pause. SABINA *is hurt.*

Sorry.

PARVIN. Do they mind that you're a beautician as well?

THAMANNA. Why would they? I do everyone's nails back at the station.

PARVIN. Even the boys?

THAMANNA. *Especially* the boys. Any time you get arrested in Tower Hamlets, check his nails. They'll be perfect. That's me, that is.

SABINA. I'll tell my brother.

PARVIN. Wouldn't they rather you were, I dunno, a professional boxer or something?

THAMANNA. It's not all about beating people up, you know.

PARVIN. Isn't it?

THAMANNA. Course not. It's about the community.

RAJNA. Leave Tham alone. I think it's great. Why can't a girl be a beautician and a policewoman?

CORE PLAYWRITING SCHEME OF WORK
Lesson 8: Objectives and Obstacles
PLTS: Creative Thinking; Reflective Learning
APP: WAF1; RAF3

---

1 Prepare for and Connect the Learning

Big question on board: what is a change in a scene?
Students write ideas on a sticky note and stick on board at front.

Discuss.

5 min

---

2 Agree Learning Objectives

- **Understand** what a change in a scene can be and how it is linked to objectives or obstacles (or both)
- **Identify** and **explain** the objectives and obstacles in a scene
- **Apply** these ideas to a scene they are currently developing

---

3 Present New Information Through the Senses

Explain to class that a shift is a change. Every moment in a play is about change. It drives the story forward.

Change in a scene can be internal (within the character) or external, and can be linked to a character's objective (what they want) or an obstacle (something that gets in the way of them getting what they want). Give two examples:

Internal	External
Change of mood	Change of job

In groups, students have 5 min to think of other internal and external changes. Other possibilities are:

Internal	External
Change of heart	Change of status
Change of mind	Change of fortune
Change of belief	Change of circumstance
Change of view	Change of allegiance
Change of affection	Change of role

Groups add new ideas to interactive whiteboard or flipchart and develop the ideas further, linking them to characters' objectives and obstacles (they could refer to their own characters or characters in extracts they have read).

15 mins

The TEEP
Learning
Cycle

---

4 Construct

Whole-class reading of extract from *Red Red Shoes*.
After reading the scene, focus on RAF3 (infer and deduce) and give the group 10 minutes' Thinking Time to consider:

What happens in the scene?
What's the main change in the scene?
Is the change internal or external (or both)?
Which character changes the most?
What are the objectives and obstacles in the scene?

Students record ideas in their books/journals; class discussion to follow based on the above questions.

25 min

---

5 Apply to Demonstrate your New Understanding

Individual work. Students begin another scene for their play and consider the following things:

What's the main change in the scene?
Is the change internal or external (or both)?
Which character changes the most?
What are the objectives and obstacles in the scene?

20 min

---

6 Review – step back and reflect on your learning

Read through the scene you have just written.
What is the state of mind of your character at the start of the scene? Happy, angry, depressed etc.
What is the state of mind of your character at the end of the scene?
Draw a symbol in your book/journal to represent how your character is feeling at the start of the scene. Draw a symbol to represent how your character is feeling at the end of the scene.
Are the symbols different? How? Why? Share ideas.

5 min

Extract

Red Red Shoes by Charles Way (*Plays for Young People*, Aurora Metro Publications Limited, reprinted 2005, p. 17)

ANNA Franvera?

FRANVERA Anna! What's the matter, what's happened?

ANNA My father says, I can no longer play at your house.

FRANVERA Why does he say that?

ANNA He says there's trouble coming. Everyone's talking about it. Haven't your parents talked about it?

FRANVERA Yes, all the time, but they said we should stay friends. They said for you to come over...

ANNA I can't. I can't. Not anymore.

FRANVERA Why not?

ANNA Last night at supper, I said you were my best friend...father slapped my face, in front of everyone. He said from now on, I can only speak to my own people. If I see you on the street I have to walk to the other side. If I don't, he will be angry, like a storm. I can't speak to you. Never.

FRANVERA Never?

ANNA Why don't you just go – leave? This is not your country – that's what he said.

FRANVERA If you don't speak to me, then I won't speak to you.

ANNA Franvera?

FRANVERA I hate you – I hate you.

CORE PLAYWRITING SCHEME OF WORK
Lesson 9: Workshop lesson
PLTS: Creative Thinking; Reflective Learning
APP: S&L AF3

1 Prepare for and Connect the Learning

As the students enter, get them to arrange the room so that all tables are pushed out of the way and the chairs are arranged in a semi-circle, so that there is a small performance area.

At this point you may want to revisit ground rules for sharing our work and how to support each other constructively. Also, good idea is, if you can, to use GCSE or AS/A2 Drama or Theatre Studies students to be the 'actors' for this lesson. **5 min**

2 Agree Learning Objectives

- **Create** and **sustain** a role through speech, gesture and movement **(if GCSE or AS/A2 students are not used)**
- **Evaluate** our own and each other's scenes

3 Present New Information Through the Senses

Explain to class that today we are going to workshop our scenes and offer feedback to each other. Remind students that we are **writing for performance** – so the writing has to have an impact on an audience, and today, we are going to be the audience. Have the following cards (or something similar) on desks:

 Great cards

Question cards

Explain to students that after you have seen someone's scene performed, you have to hold up one of each card. A great card is for something you really liked and a question card is a question you have about a character or characters or any question about the scene. It is vital that the students focus on the words and writing rather than the actors' performances here. The writers don't have to answer the questions, but instead make a note of them to refer to later. **5 min**

4 Construct

Outline expectations. Agree as group the different 'ingredients' you would be looking out for in the writing, e.g.

Conflict/tension
Objectives and obstacles
Speech patterns
Location/environment and how it affects characters
Characters' relationships
Effective openings
Etc.

5 min

The TEEP Learning Cycle

5 Apply to Demonstrate your New Understanding

Students choose one of the scenes they have written to be performed in the session today. Encourage them to pick a scene they have been struggling with, as the group can help them improve it. Take it in turns for each student to have their scene performed by their peers. After each scene is performed they receive feedback from their peers. To ensure this is kept moving smoothly, choose two 'great cards' from those that are held up for 'great comments', and three 'question cards' for questions for them to think about. Students should also identify what they think the characters' objectives (wants) were. Ensure the students are focused on the playwriting 'ingredients'. No criticism is allowed. The writer records the feedback in their books/journals. After each scene is performed, if appropriate to the scene, ask the class whether a problem, obstacle or dilemma could be included in the scene to increase the dramatic tension and take the play forward. Where possible, get the actors to improvise the scene again with the problem, obstacle or dilemma. Writers record new ideas.

If you want to assess for S&L AF3 (talking within role play and drama) you will need to prepare the students carefully beforehand, sharing the assessment criteria and modelling examples.
50 min approximately, but this really depends on the size of your group.
You may want to 'chunk' this over a few lessons.

6 Review – step back and reflect on your learning

De-brief lesson. Discuss. How was it useful? What changes do we need to make? Why?

Students record further ideas in books/journals.

5 min

You may need a few more workshop lessons depending on the size of your group. These could be run as additional sessions after school.

CORE PLAYWRITING SCHEME OF WORK

Lesson 10: Theme, Issue and Re-Writing
PLTS: Creative Thinking; Reflective Learning
APP: WAF1; WAF3

1 Prepare for and Connect the Learning

Ask students to summarise their play in one line.

Write on mini whiteboards.

Students share with whole group by holding them up.

5 min

2 Agree Learning Objectives

- **Summarise** the story of our plays
- **Evaluate** what changes and amendments need to be made to our plays

3 Present New Information Through the Senses

Students now re-visit the ideas for their plays that they had in lesson 2.
Is it still the same story or has anything changed? Why?
Now think about the story as it is.
Students write a strapline for the play (you may need to explain what this is) and write this in large letters in their books or on the front of their journals, e.g. In *The Urban Girl's Guide to Camping*, four young friends leave the city behind and head into the wilderness, but a burning secret threatens to tear their lives apart."

5 min

4 Construct

Students now write a scene-by-scene breakdown of their play, referring to their timeframe.

Refer to their washing lines again.

Are their stories complete, or are scenes missing?

10 min

The TEEP Learning Cycle

5 Apply to Demonstrate your New Understanding

Students should look at what needs to be changed in one of the scenes now other decisions have been made, and make changes and rewrites.

Think about the questions the students asked during the workshop process – have they been answered within the play?

Complete additions and changes for homework if not completed in the lesson.

See Noël Greig's book *Playwriting: A Practical Guide* for further ideas.

40 min

6 Review – step back and reflect on your learning

Planning ahead. The plays should now be ready to be performed.
Think about how the students' work can be shared in school.
Could there be a writing festival?
Could the plays be shared in assemblies or at parents' evenings?
Is there a community event where the plays could be performed?
This could be developed further, with students taking on the roles of director, stage manager, lighting and set designers, marketing etc., and could become a cross-curricular project with further opportunities for the development of the Personal, Learning and Thinking Skills.
Plays or scenes can now be assessed for writing. We suggest you assess for WAF3 (organise and present whole texts effectively, sequencing and structuring information, events and ideas) and WAF1 (write imaginative, interesting and thoughtful texts).

10 min

3

Special Educational Needs (SEN) SoW

Introduction to SEN SoW

This SoW is to be used with students who have low levels of writing ability and it has been used with students with a wide range of educational needs. Students who have had specific physical, sensory, behavioural and/ or autistic conditions have developed plays that have helped to tap into their imagination and create rich stories. Moreover, the SoW also helped to develop students' independent decision-making processes, enabling them to make their own choices and reach their own decisions. The SoW can also be used in mainstream schools with students working at National Curriculum level 1 or below. Please see the National Curriculum level descriptors for Assessing Pupil Progress in English for further information (see bibliography for web address).

The SoW follows the same principles as the others found in this book and applies the core basic ingredients of playwriting, adapted to the needs of the students. More teaching input is needed for this, and we recommend a teacher to lead the workshops and another to act as a scribe. Other teaching support will be required for the breakout writing sessions as appropriate to the individual needs of the students within each group.

The teacher's role is to lead the lessons and draw out the ideas from the students. The more performative the approach the better, in order for the students to see their ideas acted out and come to life throughout the process, but teachers should use their own understanding of their groups and professional judgement with this. The role of the scribe is to document the ideas that emerge during the workshops and to help to shape the play. The scribe's role is detailed in the case study below, highlighting where they need to be and what information they need to have gathered at each stage of the process. The scribe will have a role after the fifth workshop to put all of the information and writing that has been generated into a 'script'. The final script doesn't necessarily have to resemble a fully developed stage play, but it does have to have a clear structure and scenes within it where all of the action is outlined in detail. The final script could allow room for improvisation but the action will have been predetermined by the students at all times, retaining their role as 'playwright', having made all of the decisions along the way.

The workshop stage is crucial in this programme to bring the characters to life to facilitate and deepen their histories, stories and connections with each other. The more the writers can participate in this, the more sense of ownership and a stronger narrative for the play will be evident. This stage needs to be recorded, as a useful record for the scribe to record and shape the final script, but also for the students to have as a tool to make decisions about the final shape and structure of their play.

Visual aids such as images, artefacts and other stimuli are used in the other SoW to engage students and prompt and support ideas. They are used extensively in this SoW and we encourage teachers to use artefacts already in the school building as a way of getting immediate responses from the group. Familiarity and repetition can be vital when working with students with special educational needs and can help to contribute to the success of this SoW.

The use of routine is important, so lessons should begin in the same way every time, and a pattern aids this sense of security and the need to feel structured in what the students are learning. If the teacher leading the session isn't the group's usual teacher, it is vital to spend some time with their usual teacher and the group to familiarise themselves with the students. As with all students, the students always need to know the 'bigger picture' and what their learning journey is. If an idea is introduced in one workshop, it has to be followed through in subsequent workshops. Encouraging students to tap into their own vocabulary and understanding of words is vital, but if necessary, words can be provided for students when they are asked to describe their characters. Displaying these around the room is a way of enabling the students to find these words for themselves. A list of words and emotion cards could be provided as a point of reference to go back to when applying this to their own characters.

The SoW allows students to express their ideas in three ways. If they have difficulty writing, they can 'write' by drawing or sculpting ideas in modelling clay. All of the ideas and pictures should be recorded via photos and used as reference and to stimulate further ideas throughout.

This SoW will challenge some around the notion of the role of the writer as the person who puts pen to paper. The writer here is the generator of the ideas and the subsequent development of these ideas through the key decisions made to guide the dramatic action and relationships of the characters within the play. The scribe is to remain truthful to these ideas, is to reproduce these back to the writers, and is to retain the energy and tone that is present throughout the workshops.

Examples of texts to use

We have included an extract from Noël Greig's play *Tin Soldier*, which is published by Aurora Metro Publications, to be used in the first lesson. The book includes two other plays that would be suitable for using with this SoW, and reference to *Hood in the Wood*, also by Noël Greig, is found in the second lesson. A wealth of plays are being produced that would be suitable for use in this SoW, but sadly there is very little published material. The work in this anthology, *The Tin Soldier and other plays*, has been produced on the stage by Tangere Arts, a theatre company that tours work for children.

Case study and description of the role of the scribe

Calthorpe Specialist Sports College is an all-age (2–19) co-educational Special School near the centre of Birmingham and provides facilities for children with special educational needs. We worked with a group of 11 students aged 11–15 years, some of whom were diagnosed with varying degrees of autism and/or other multiple, complex learning difficulties and emotional and behavioural problems. Some members of the group had very severe autism and could not communicate by speech. The group had varying reading abilities from age five plus, but all were working at level 1 or below for English in relation to National Curriculum levels. Kathy Joyce from the Shysters Theatre Company led the lessons and playwright Alex Jones acted as scribe. If there is a budget available for this programme, you could employ a playwright in the role of the scribe. Most theatre companies will have contact with playwrights, and contacting their education/learning and participation and/or literary departments is a way of connecting with them. Going to see a play that is suitable for that age range is a good way of introducing the SoW to students. This can be used as a reference point to what they are doing by writing their own play.

The first lesson for the scribe will be a process of documenting and listing ideas that emerge from the group. The exercise following the extract from *Tin Soldier* will produce a list of ideas leading into developing these further in the Construct phase of lesson 4. In this phase of the lesson the teacher is encouraging the students to link ideas together and think about how objects could be the start of a story. The focus should shift to personal experiences and connections to objects. The students at Calthorpe were full of ideas, and those more able to communicate orally immediately came up with the start of many stories. Their responses were a mixture of the real and the magical, with insects and animals already beginning to emerge as future characters. Some of their ideas included:

1.   A journey in a jungle.
2.   Rowing a boat on the sea.
3.   A box of cornflakes in a kitchen with a spider and a worm inside.

4. A complete set of pigs; mummy, daddy, baby girl and baby boy pig watching television.
5. People Island where the mangoes grow.
6. Wasps' nests.
7. A trip to Paris and a ride up the Eiffel Tower.

The box of cornflakes that was used as an object in the Story Box had its own story and characters attached to it as outlined above. The cereal package in the kitchen led to the set of pigs that started their day watching television in the kitchen. All these became characters in the final play, and a mango in the Story Box generated the later location, People Island. The scribe should now have generated a long list of objects from the box, and sentences and fragments of ideas that can all be used in the play and to generate further ideas.

This list should be used in lesson 2 to begin their character work. At Calthorpe the characters that began to inhabit the play they were creating included:

1. Dolphin
2. Monkey
3. Lion
4. Spider
5. Octopus
6. Family of pigs, the blue spotted pigs
7. Princess
8. Massive crocodile
9. Cowboy

Lesson 3 should encourage students to put their characters in locations they would not normally find them in, and this is a key moment in the pulling together of everyone's ideas into a core narrative for one play. The students will decide where the central action of the play is located, and at Calthorpe this became People Island, an idea from the earlier lesson, where the mangoes grow.

The narrative began to emerge in the workshop session with the actors. The scribe will need to have the list of characters and all of the ideas already generated at the workshop lesson. At the end of each improvised scenario as outlined in phase 5 of the fourth lesson in the SoW the scribe will write down and/or record what happens in that scene. All of the decisions will have been made by the students. At Calthorpe the following things began to emerge;

1. The cowboy's journey on his motorbike. He met the wasp, the rabbit and the pig along the way.
2. Laura the Lion was in Africa and she came into contact with the crocodile, the lion, the ghost, the dolphin, the man in the moon and the cowboy on his motorbike.
3. The princess tale was created and she met the shark, the dolphin, the bear and the big octopus.

Lesson 5 is about making sense of all of these encounters and creating a coherent structure for the play. The telling of this will probably already have started organically through the workshop lesson. At Calthorpe they went back to their original ideas to find a route into this, and it is vital that all of this information is still readily accessible throughout all of the lessons. They decided to create a play that was about a group of students telling each other a tale when the lights went out after a journey they had all had to Ogwen Cottage. This became the framing device for the whole play leading the story to People Island, a more magical habitat that allowed the encounters between the family of pigs, the cowboy and the wasp before finding the Princess of Birmingham.

Example of students' work

A group of students were in bed after an activities day in Wales when they began to tell each other stories . . .

Extract from: *From Ogwen Cottage to the Oka Sea* by students from Calthorpe School and Alex Jones

D I know, let's tell a story no one's ever heard.

A Great!

B Brilliant!

D Something pretty with princesses.

A Nah, with a crocodile.

B Lions and tigers.

C Dolphins

E Cowboys!

D There was an ocean.

A A beach.

B A jungle.

E A desert.

C A stagnant, slimy green pool that stinks!

D Yeah, just like your smelly socks!

(LAUGHTER)

A (SPOTS A BOX) Hey, wait, look – there's a box!

B What's that doing there?

C Never seen that before.

D Know what?

E What?

D I think it's magic.

A A magic box?

B Wow!

C Wonder what's inside?

D Know what?

E What?

A I think our story's in there.

B Hey, could be if it's magic.

E Could be happy.

C Could be tragic.

D Could be a boat on a sea.

A A cow in a field.

C *A cow?*

B A cow called Alex.

A No, a cow called Cami.

E Or a cowboy on a motorbike out for a ride.

D Only one way to find out – let's look inside.

THEY ALL CLIMB OUT OF BED AND GO TO THE BOX. D CAREFULLY LIFTS THE LID AND PEERS INSIDE.

D Oh my goodness!

The scribe will gather all of the information into the play, and the extract highlights how every word and idea that the students come up with can find its way into their play.

Lesson plans, resources and extract for SEN SoW

Lesson 1 (Page 77)
Resources

- Extract (in resource) from *Tin Soldier*
- The 'Story Box' – the Story Box should be a large box with lots of different kinds of artefacts, props and objects that could start generating ideas for a story. The box can include everyday objects (e.g. a bus pass; a cereal packet) and should connect to the students' own experiences. This could include pictures/objects linked to places and locations they might have been to on school trips (e.g. the Eiffel Tower) or places they may have researched in lessons in school (e.g. the Amazon rainforest)
- IWB or flipchart for scribe to record ideas
- Resources to enable students of different abilities to be able to 'write' in different ways – e.g. pens and paper, symbols or pictures, classroom displays, word mats, picture dictionaries etc.

Lesson 2 (Page 79)
Resources

- Story Box
- Extract (see suggested reading list) from 'A Tasty Tale – the true story of Hansel and Gretel' by Noël Greig (*Tin Soldier and other plays*)
- Materials for writing, drawing and sculpting (e.g. modelling clay etc.)
- Signs, symbols and images used in school to support communication and learning

Lesson 3 (Page 80)

Resources

- Photographs of the students' characters from last lesson
- Story Box
- Three different 'zoned' areas of the room – see lesson plan for detailed advice on resources
- Materials for writing, drawing and sculpting (e.g. modelling clay etc.)
- Pictures/photographs of locations familiar to the students

Lesson 4 (Page 81)

Resources

- Space to perform scenes
- Digital camera
- Video recorder
- Photographs of students' characters from last couple of lessons
- Story Box

Lesson 5 (Page 82)

Resources

- Photographs of actors in role as students' characters from last lesson
- Still shots of scenes from last lesson
- 'Zoned' areas of room – 'Beginning', 'Middle' and 'End' – see lesson plan for further details

SEN PLAYWRITING SCHEME OF WORK
Lesson 1: Stories
PLTS: Creative Thinking
APP: WAF3 Level 1
P Scale Writing: P2ii; P3i; P4; P5; P6; P7; P8

---

1 Prepare for and Connect the Learning

This SoW will need to be led by a teacher alongside a 'scribe' at all times. NB – the role of the scribe is for an adult, not a student, in this SoW. Please see introduction for further information and checklist on the crucial role of the scribe. Additional teaching assistants required as necessary, depending on the group.

Welcome. Share 'bigger picture' for SoW – how we're going to write our own group play. What is a play? Question group's understanding of what a play is and experiences of theatre both in and outside school.

---

2 Agree Learning Objectives

Contextualise SoW.
- **Describe** an idea/memory/ thought
- **Explain** our idea/memory/thought in more detail

---

3 Present New Information Through the Senses

Read extract of *Tin Soldier* by Noel Greig as a group (see resources).
Check ideas – what could be in the box? Share ideas and scribe documents them. Link to learning objectives.

---

4 Construct

Link to extract and introduce the Story Box. The Story Box should be a large box with lots of different kinds of artefacts, props and objects that could start generating ideas for a story.

Link to the extract read earlier in the lesson: so what IS in the box?

This can include everyday objects (e.g. a bus pass; a cereal packet) and should connect to the students' own experiences. This could include pictures/objects linked to places and locations they might have been to on school trips (e.g. the Eiffel Tower) or places they may have researched in lessons in school (e.g. the Amazon rainforest). Students should take it in turns to draw objects/props out from the box. Teacher should encourage students to link ideas and think about how the objects could be part of a story and the starting point for a play. What happens? Who does this belong to? Why?
e.g. Did you have cereal for breakfast?
What happened on your way to school?
Did you catch the bus? Who with?
Have you been to Paris?
Have you been on a school trip? Where did you go? Etc....
All of the answers should be recorded by the scribe, as these are characters and journeys that will emerge in the play.

A distinction should be made between the teacher and the scribe here. The teacher is the leader of the session – the one acting it out and drawing the ideas out of the student – and the scribe is to document what students come up with at this stage.

The teacher leading should try to 'act back' to the students what their ideas are, to really try to bring to life what they are thinking. The scribe should record the students' ideas throughout on the IWB.

The TEEP Learning Cycle

---

5 Apply to Demonstrate your New Understanding

Explain to the class that we have now begun to describe our ideas/memories/thoughts by speaking (link to first learning objective) and we are now going to try and describe and explain them (second learning objective) in more detail by writing. Based on the ideas from the Story Box, students should now chose their favourite idea/memory/thought linked to the object/prop and describe:

- What time of day it is
- What the location/place is like
- Who is there.

'Writing' will differ depending on the ability of your group. All students should be encouraged to think about and discuss what they intend to write, ahead of writing it. Those students working at the lower end of the P scale for Writing could be encouraged to use symbols/images/signing to indicate ideas, and may sometimes be able to anticipate what comes next by gesturing, vocalising or making a choice between two pictures/symbols. Some students will be able to write in full or partial sentences, and those students working at Level 1 should be able to sequence their events and ideas in appropriate order, with support. Those students who are not able to write in full or partial sentences should be encouraged to rehearse and then dictate a sentence for an adult to scribe or select symbols or pictures to make a sentence by pointing or eye-pointing. Students could also be encouraged to use classroom displays, word mats, picture dictionaries and each other to support independent writing.

---

6 Review – step back and reflect on your learning

Share ideas – either students or teaching assistants reading out students' work and ideas. Scribe records ideas on IWB. Have we achieved our learning objectives? How?

By the end of this lesson the scribe should have everything documented in a list ready for next lesson.

Extract

Tin Soldier by **Noël Greig** (Adapted from *The Steadfast Tin Soldier* by Hans Christian Andersen) (*Tin Soldier and other plays for children*), 2010, Aurora Metro Publications, p. 13

There's a room

And it's lit

By the flickering flames

Of the logs on the fire

In the grate

There's a box

And a boy

And a birthday

And a crate of new toys for the boy

Trumpets and drums

Games and paints

Books and battleships

And a castle

What a lot!

But the box

What's in the box?

SEN PLAYWRITING SCHEME OF WORK

Lesson 2: Characters

PLTS: Creative Thinking; Reflective Learning

APP: WAF1 Level 1

P Scale Writing: P2ii; P3i; P4; P5; P6; P7; P8

1 Prepare for and Connect the Learning

Welcome group. Explain again to the group what the SoW is about and that we're writing our own group play. Remind group about extract read last lesson. What were our ideas from the Story Box? Teacher uses list that scribe prepared last lesson. Students support ideas with symbols and flash cards and other work from last lesson.

2 Agree Learning Objectives

- **Identify** your character
- _Describe_ how your character is feeling

3 Present New Information Through the Senses

Introduce a character that the students are familiar with. This could be a character from a story they know well. Question the group about what we know about the character, and what we know from what he/she says or how they act. Alternatively you could read an extract from 'A Tasty Tale – the true story of Hansel and Gretel' from *Tin Soldier and other plays for Children* by Noël Greig (see reading list).

Read as a group from 'He boasted and bragged' until 'in the face of great danger'. Ensure you don't mention that this is about Hansel and Gretel so the students do not get too caught up in familiar stories that may have too great an influence on their own, new ones. What do we think about this character? What do we find out about him from what he says?

Remind group (or ask a student to remind the group) about our own ideas from last lesson from the Story Box. What were they? Who were the characters in our ideas/memories/thoughts? Today we are going to think in more detail about the characters and what their personalities are and how they are feeling. Are they boastful and bragging like this character? Or are they quiet and meek? How else could they be?

4 Construct

Revisit each student's ideas from last lesson, with assistance from TAs. What time of day was it? What was the location/place? Who was the character? Use the Story Box if necessary to help support ideas. Scribe records any further ideas from students as and when they appear.

5 Apply to Demonstrate your New Understanding

Explain to class that now we have identified our characters (reference first learning objective), we are going to describe our characters in detail and how they are feeling (second learning objective). Teacher leader encourages students to think about their own characters' personality and emotions through Think, Pair, Share – think on own first (or with help from TA); then share your ideas with a partner; then share with the rest of the group. Three or four minutes' thinking time on their own (or with a teaching assistant), pair up with a partner to discuss and share ideas for another three or four minutes and then share with the rest of the group. Students should be supported throughout with symbols and signs for feelings and emotions and also encouraged to refer to key words and wall displays, as well as picture dictionaries.

Students now move on to deepening their ideas about their characters through developing character sketches. They are given three options: to write about, draw or sculpt their character with modelling materials. This could also be carried out as a collage. The image or description of their character must have the following:

- A name for their character
- The age of their character
- At least one emotion for their character (use of adjectives)
- A word or sentence to describe how the character moves (use of adverbs)

Again, differentiate support as necessary and provide students at lower end of the P scale with opportunities to convey their ideas through using signs, symbols and images, as well as sculpting their character. Sculptures and collages could be labelled with adjectives and adverbs to describe the character in more detail. Students working at P8 and Level 1 should be encouraged to write in full sentences.

The teacher/scribe should take digital images of the students' work as a means of recording the 'writing'. If possible, transfer these images to the IWB to share at the end of the lesson.

6 Review – step back and reflect on your learning

If teachers and TAs have been able to assemble them in time, photographs of character images, sculptures and writing should scroll through on IWB for students to view. Alternatively, students walk around room as at a 'gallery', viewing their peers' work. Have we achieved our learning objectives? How do we know? Use the Thumb Tool to ascertain whether students feel they have achieved the learning objective: thumbs up – yes I have; thumb to the side – not sure; thumbs down – no I haven't. You can then target questions (and support) accordingly.

By the end of this lesson the scribe should have documented a list of characters in the play.

The TEEP Learning Cycle

SEN PLAYWRITING SCHEME OF WORK

Lesson 3: Location, setting, atmosphere

PLTS: Creative Thinking

APP: WAF1 Level 1

P Scale Writing: P2ii; P3i; P4; P5; P6; P7; P8

1 Prepare for and Connect the Learning

Welcome group. Scrolling photographs of group's characters on IWB and stuck around room.

Remind class of the stories and characters that emerged last lesson. Use the Story Box and lists from the scribe if required.

This lesson is about finding a place where all these characters could be – to bring them together into one play.

NB – This lesson really enables the students to immerse themselves in the world of the play. Depending on the time you have available and the size of your group, you may want to split this lesson over two lessons. The flexibility of the TEEP cycle enables you to do this quite easily.

2 Agree Learning Objectives

- **Describe and explain** the location, setting and atmosphere of our stories

3 Present New Information Through the Senses

Explain to the group that we are now going to make decisions about where our story will be set, what the name of the place or country where it is set will be, what the atmosphere is like, what the time of day is and what the weather's like etc. First of all we need to have some ideas:

Have the room 'zoned' into different areas. Students spend about 10 minutes in each 'zone' experiencing different stimuli:

Location zone – have lots of different stimuli in this area for the students to stimulate ideas for locations, e.g. a tray of sand with seashells; a bucket of dried leaves; images of the moon and space with accompanying music; sounds of lapping/roaring waves and images of the sea; a class display about a location they have researched previously (e.g. the Amazon rainforest). Ensure that in this zone are also flashcards of the names of different locations; students can also be encouraged to use the internet to research them further.

Atmosphere zone – this zone should have different stimuli that help to evoke different atmospheres, e.g. headsets could be set up where students listen to calming, peaceful music; other headsets could have forceful, agitated, exciting music playing. If you work in a special school and have a sensory room, use this to evoke different atmospheres through the sounds and projections. Other musical instruments could be introduced to evoke different atmospheres – e.g. tinkling bells or thumping drums (you may want the music room to be your atmosphere zone).

Time and weather zone – this zone should utilise existing class displays or interactive games that enable students to tell the time and describe the weather. It could also be accompanied by laptops and, if possible, the projector showing images of different types of weather (e.g. sunshine, hurricanes, thunderstorms etc.).

All zones should be supported by teachers and TAs.

The TEEP Learning Cycle

4 Construct

This is a turning point within the SoW where the individual ideas start to amalgamate into one story. Encourage the students to link the ideas they have just experienced to the one character they chose and developed last lesson. Ask the question: in which location would you find your character?

Scribe records any ideas.

5 Apply to Demonstrate your New Understanding

Students now apply what they experienced earlier in the lesson to their own characters and ideas. They write, draw, sculpt or create a collage in response to the following questions. These should be displayed on the IWB but all teachers/TAs should also have copies:

- Where is your character? (location)
- What is the name of the place or country?
- What is the atmosphere like?
- What time of day is it?
- What is the weather like?

Encourage students to refer back to the decisions they made in lesson 1 (use photos of their work from this lesson to help) and to decide whether any changes have been made and why. As per all previous lessons, students should be given the opportunity to convey ideas through signs and symbols if necessary.

6 Review – step back and reflect on your learning

The group now need to make a decision about where the play is set – a place where all their characters would find themselves and where all their characters tell a story. All their ideas could be included. In the case study example included it was Ogwen Cottage, a place where all the students had been on a school trip and had experienced. So this decision really depends on your group of students and their experiences. For this phase of the lesson we suggest you collect a number of different images of places familiar to all the students and put them into a scrolling PPT and stick the images around the room. The students could then decide where they would like their play to be set by standing next to the image they like best. The most popular image wins. All the students' ideas for their own stories and locations can still be included; this is just the central location for all the characters and where the stories begin.

The scribe should then document the agreed location for the play.

SEN PLAYWRITING SCHEME OF WORK

Lesson 4: Workshop lesson –
Deepening the Story
PLTS: Creative Thinking; Teamwork
APP: S&L AF3 Level 1
P Scale Writing: P2ii; P3i; P4; P5; P6; P7; P8

1 Prepare for and Connect the Learning

NB – you will need a still camera and video recorder for this lesson.

This lesson is about putting the characters into different scenarios to find out more about them, their relationships and creating the narrative from this.

Scrolling photographs of group's characters from last lesson on IWB and/or stuck around room. Welcome group. Have a pre-prepared performance space in the room. Explain to the students why the space is different and how we are going to get to know our characters from last lesson a bit better today by acting them out. Establish with group what this means.

If you work in a school with GCSE or AS/A2 Drama or Theatre Studies students, a great idea is for them to be the 'actors' for this lesson. If not, or if you work in a special school with lots of TA support, your more confident students, as well as TAs and teachers, will be the 'actors'. Less confident students could be encouraged to join in as the lesson progresses.

2 Agree Learning Objectives

- **Explain** how different characters move, speak and behave, how they react to each other and why
- **Create** and sustain a role (this is an extension objective for those students who are able to do this)

3 Present New Information Through the Senses

Ensure all group know who the characters are. Scribe records on IWB if necessary. Revisit each image of every student's character. Repetition and familiarity are important here.

4 Construct

Interactive Q&A session between actors and students. Actors question the students on how the characters move and behave. This should be the starting point for the actors, rather than the actors imposing their interpretations of how the characters would move and interact.

The TEEP
Learning Cycle

6 Review – step back and reflect on your learning

The scribe revisits the stories that have emerged.
Read out.

Explain that next lesson we will 'map' the story of the play and what happens. Does anyone have any ideas now?

5 Apply to Demonstrate your New Understanding

NB – You will need a video recorder for this phase of the lesson to record the improvised scenes and revisit them next lesson.

You now need to begin to deepen the story in more detail as a group. The actors will develop and physicalise the characters with the students. Introduce the location for the play that the students decided on last lesson. Choose two characters and put them together in this location. Ask the students to make a few decisions before they act it out, e.g.: Have the characters met before? Where are they going? Are they happy, sad etc.? What happens to them after meeting the other character? Does this meeting change them in any way? How do the characters speak?

Make sure each character meets the others and play around with this. Put the characters you wouldn't immediately think of meeting together and see what ideas the students come up with.

Ask the students what happens, and begin to develop the story through other characters. Act this out.

What the characters say and any other details that begin to emerge about location should be recorded. The Story Box could also be used here to introduce obstacles and objects into the developing stories by the student, teacher or actor choosing something from the box and the students asked how it might affect what the character wants or where they're going. Those students who cannot communicate in full or partial sentences could be encouraged to point to or indicate objects in the Story Box or symbols that they would like to be included in the story.

Always refer back (and get the students to refer back) to the character from last lesson to ensure continuity and linking and connecting back to prior learning.

It is very important that the scribe records the students' decisions about the story and what happens. At the end of this lesson the group should have a clear picture of what the story of the play is.

NB – it is vital that the scribe records all of this – the decisions before the improvisation and what happens during it – including the dialogue.

At the end of each scenario the scribe writes down what happens – for an example of this see the case study we have included (the cowboy's journey on his motorbike. He met the wasp, the rabbit and the pig along the way.)

SEN PLAYWRITING SCHEME OF WORK

Lesson 5: Mapping the Story and Final Decisions

PLTS: Creative Thinking; Teamwork

APP: S&L AF3 Level 1

P Scale Writing: P2ii; P3i; P4; P5; P6; P7; P8

1 Prepare for and Connect the Learning

This lesson is about mapping out the story and pulling all the students' ideas into one narrative.

Welcome students and actors, who will join this lesson again. What decisions did we make last lesson about location and characters? The scribe should have the list of information and dialogue ready from last lesson.

2 Agree Learning Objectives

- **Create** the journey for our story and **explain** what happens to the different characters

3 Present New Information Through the Senses

This is a quick activity to remind the students of characters and decisions that they have made:

Have pre-prepared cards created that are laminated photos of your actors in role. Do a 'pick a card' activity where a student volunteer picks a card and explains who the character is; what they want; what has happened to them; who they have met; how they speak etc.

4 Construct

Explain to the group that we know our characters really well, and now we are going to decide the order of events for our play. First we have to revisit what happens. Show the group the recording of last lesson's improvised scenes.

NB – For the next phase of the lesson you will need some still shots from these scenes from last lesson, preferably labelled with the characters' names and a brief explanation of what's happening in the scene.

The TEEP Learning Cycle

5 Apply to Demonstrate your New Understanding

'Zone' your IWB or classroom into different areas – Beginning, Middle and End. Explain to the group that these areas represent the different stages of our play. We are now going to make some decisions about when the events/encounters we improvised last lesson (and have just watched) will take place in the story of our play.

Teacher leads: take one still shot from the scenes. Show it to the group and ask them whether this would take place at the beginning, middle or end of the play and why. Group discussion and decision made by mutual agreement or voting where it should go and why. Class discussion. Teacher or TA sticks it on wall in appropriate area (Beginning, Middle or End). Repeat process with all still shots from scenes. Scribe documents everything so the story is clear.

6 Review – step back and reflect on your learning

The scribe revisits the story that has emerged. Read out. Scribe explains that he/she will put all the group's ideas together (please see notes for scribe for further details about how to do this). The next, final lesson should be a performance of the play. You could decide to perform it as you wish – for parents and carers; for the rest of the school; as part of an Arts Day or community celebration etc.

4

English as an Additional Language (EAL) SoW

Introduction to EAL SoW

This SoW is primarily written for students newly-arrived to the UK, who speak English as an additional language (EAL). The SoW can also be adapted for use with students who are not newly-arrived but still speak English as an additional language. Newly-arrived students on induction programmes can write a play together, or this can work with a mixed-ability group: newly-arrived students and students who have gone into the mainstream classes and have more advanced English. There is no limit to the number of first languages that can work together; the SOW is designed to incorporate multiple voices and cultures through its narrative. The play will be shaped by the individual experiences of the students. These lessons have been designed to last longer than the average 70-minute lesson, and we suggest two hours because the students may need extra time to understand and develop their ideas through the activities. We have found this immersion time to be more effective and less disjointed for EAL learners.

The common experience amongst these students is travel and journeys. They have all been on different routes to find themselves at their particular school. No one experience will be the same and no one school will have the same countries, cultures and languages together in one room. They all, though, will have a class of students that has travelled, often many miles, to be sitting in the same room and are learning how to communicate in a second or third language.

The aim of this programme is to increase their vocabulary and confidence in being able to listen and understand English, and in writing and speaking in English by writing a collaborative play. The SoW is designed to slowly build up their recognition of vocabulary and modes of communication through the development of a narrative that they can all shape. There is a clear end result to this work that shows tangible signs of their achievement and development of language skills through their individual contributions.

The group will develop the play collaboratively but all students will input independently throughout the process. There are constant activities that also act as an indicator to the teacher of the level of comprehension within the group and subsequently the progress of the students' language skills. These are primarily through the use of questions that the students ask about the story and characters, and they have a dual role in deepening the story and opening the play into areas previously not explored (reference lesson 4, phases 3 and 6; lesson 5, phase 4).

The emphasis is not about correcting grammar or spelling but about increasing the confidence of the students to speak, write and communicate in English and their fluency in this new language. The use of whole-class teaching and modelling of writing through writing group scenes is a method employed to build the confidence of the students to later facilitate independent and smaller group writing (reference lesson 2, phase 5; lesson 3, phases 4 and 5).

This SoW incorporates all of the elements to be found in other SoW but arranged in a different order. The starting point is using location and environment to find the narrative and to deepen their story and grasp of English. This entry into their play has been selected because it focuses on their strengths and celebrates their knowledge of the world. It engages them with familiar places and vocabulary to allow them easier access into the world of the play by promoting confidence through their often greater knowledge of the locations and environments that the characters of the play will inhabit. This generates a sense of ownership and promotes self-confidence in English through creative expression. The SoW is designed to encourage students to develop their writing and ideas and to incorporate these ideas into the core narrative. (Reference lesson 2, phase 3). It might be necessary to agree with the group or decide a maximum number of countries the character can go to during the course of the play to keep it achievable and manageable. We recommend four or five; any more than six in one scheme of work could create problems.

The teaching of this SoW needs to be clear, and lots of examples should be used before each phase of the lesson. In our experience, using many extra examples and concrete artefacts and pictures to support ideas/concepts is beneficial to ensure that ideas are understood. It is often necessary to be explicit and over-explain and repeat the vocabulary already introduced; teachers will use their professional judgement to ascertain this. Teachers need to choose their questions about the scenes and characters carefully to ensure that they push the narrative forward, to help enable the group to make the decisions that react to their ideas and shape them into dramatic action. Words from their first languages will also inevitably find their way into the text and should be valued and celebrated.

The aural assessment

An aural assessment has been incorporated into the SoW at the beginning and end. This is to enable schools to ascertain what words in English students can identify by listening, and then to measure improvement by assessing again at the end. The listening exercise should be read out by the teacher twice at the beginning of the first workshop and the students will fill in a multiple-choice visual questionnaire in order for their level of comprehension to be assessed. This should be repeated at the end of the SoW to enable teachers to assess the progress of their students. An example of the assessment form can be found in the resources section of this chapter. The aural assessment has also been incorporated to introduce the theme of journeys and associated vocabulary as well as the beginning of the writing process. The sample listening exercise is about a boy getting ready to go on a secret journey and includes vocabulary such as:

train station
trip
bicycle
aeroplane
ticket office
bus
platform.

Teachers can write their own listening exercise to be used as the aural assessment, using their knowledge of their students' ability. The exercise should include information about a character and opportunities to develop relationships with other characters. We are given some facts about Simon in the sample exercise and ideas for other characters such as Mohammed, his sister and his mother. The character must be getting ready to go on a journey though, leaving multiple possibilities for what could happen to him later on. This character can be used as the example in lesson 1, phase 2 if necessary.

Case study with EAL students at Harborne Academy, Birmingham, UK

Harborne Academy in Birmingham developed a play with students on their induction EAL programme and students that had gone into the mainstream classes. This was therefore a mixed-ability group of year 7s and 8s, and the group consisted of around 12 students and more than six different nationalities. The number of students varied from session to session, with students leaving the school and entering the programme at different stages. The programme was led by Fiona King, Education Officer at Birmingham Repertory Theatre and was supported by Damian Topczewski, teacher of EAL at Harborne Academy.

The map exercise in lesson 2 provided a rich starting point for the narrative, and a wealth of material through their own journeys emerged which demonstrated all of the countries they had travelled to between them:

Somalia	Saudi Arabia
Kenya	Egypt
Afghanistan	Albania
England	Poland
Sweden	Turkey
Pakistan	Ethiopia
USA	Iran
Holland	Greece
France	Spain
Hong Kong	Jamaica
Canada.	

This led to sentences and anecdotes being created about their journeys, using some of the vocabulary already introduced:

'One day on a bus from Poland to England, travelled through France because they got stuck because of the ash cloud and had to get the bus.'

'Angola to Poland by bus then airbus from Portugal to Spain.'

The process of then making it a character's journey depersonalised the material but incorporated all the words and journeys that had been used thus far, developing the following journey for Ali, their protagonist;

1. Character goes by plane from England to USA for business. Ali is an engineer and is going to show some designs for the new World Trade Centre.
2. Plane to Brazil for a holiday.
3. Visits family in Turkey.
4. Goes to Somalia to visit his friend from primary school.
5. Goes to Madagascar with his friend by boat to take some pictures.

6.   Goes to Afghanistan to buy jewellery.
7.   Returns to England.

In the third lesson they decided as a group that the scene in America would have two characters in a burger restaurant in the USA waiting for Ali. Ania was a Polish architect and Sarah the manager of the World Trade Centre. The first line:

Ania: 'Boring...'

could easily have led the group down a dead end but the question asked by the teacher was, 'Is Ania polite or is she rude?' This prompted a conversation about Sarah and Ania and their differences in personality and approaches to the business meeting. Sarah was more accommodating towards Ali's lateness, and created tension and subsequently moved the scene forward, creating dramatic action.

The postcard writing in lesson 4 not only helped the teacher to assess the level of the students' comprehension but acted as a resource for material to be included in the narrative. The postcards were all later used in the play and these helped to link the story, and to ensure that every student saw their writing in the text. Their confidence in writing English had developed by this point to where all the students felt able to complete the exercise and read their postcards to the group. This was the first time that every student contributed in this way, and one girl who had recently arrived in the UK and had not previously spoken, ran to the front of the class to read her postcard. A sense of pride and ownership of the project was clear by this stage. The writing of the postcards was supported, as the students were provided with starter sentences. Those students with more advanced English were encouraged to write independently without the aid of the starter sentences. This is important in ensuring that the writing "scaffolded" in this way does not become a crutch.

The words that the students came up with about the specific locations and environments found their way into the play and helped to deepen the story, linking them back to their previous research using repetition again to reinforce comprehension. The words were a mixture of locations and environments, which later translated into decisions they would make about the narrative.

Brazil

Rio	big buildings
statues and monuments	football stadium
celebration	colourful
full of people	really loud
Mexican waves	beach
tropical forest	dark
lots of trees	animals
water	scary snakes
lakes	jungle
rainy	humid

Turkey

mosque	Istanbul
hospital	harbour
fresh air	boats
peaceful	fish, fish, fish
cafes	ships
sea	holiday
relaxed	sand
sun	crowded
pollution	hot
traffic	police
homeless people	

Somalia

hot	mosque
Mogadishu	dangerous people and cars
noisy	shops
tomatoes	markets

fresh fruit	vegetables
headscarf	port of Bosaso
fish	tradition
dangerous boats	pirates

Madagascar

islandsand	pictures
lemurs	quiet and noisy
lots of trees	no big hotels
wild animals	a roof made of leaves
relaxed	

Afghanistan

desert	Kabul
houses	cold winters
windy	old buildings
markets to buy dresses (jalabia)	hijab.

What can seem like an arduous task around defining location and environment actually releases the ideas for the narrative of the play and enables every student to write and speak English.

The sticky note strategy in lesson 5 after the talk booklets is a great way to keep assessing the students' understanding and progress throughout rather than just the one test at the beginning and end of the SoW. By this stage the increased confidence was evident. Students who had previously found writing exercises troublesome for fear of getting it wrong, were ready to give it a go. As with the learning of any new language, going past the fear of getting it wrong is a clear indicator that comprehension and confidence have increased. The students were also adding their own languages in some scenes, deepening the story.

Example of students' work

This is an example of one of the scenes and demonstrates how the postcards were used to give a sense of the bigger journey of the play:

> Dear Damian, I am writing to you from Somalia. It was a good day. And hot. It was great. I feel so bad because the pirates try to kill me and my friends. Something happened the other day. Go to see how the road was, it was not good. I saw pirates they try to kill me. It made me feel angry. Hope to see you soon! Ali

and to link scenes together and begin new ones:

> Dear Mahlet, I am writing to you from Madagascar. It is hot today. I'm going to the beach in a minute and drink some coconut water. I feel happy because it's so quiet where I am. Something happened to me the other day. I went to the forest and I found so many big scary animals. It made me feel scary. Hope to see you soon! Ali

Madagascar – 3am and it is cold and his friend has just arrived in Madagascar after being on a boat for one day. Ali called his girlfriend.

Ali: Guess what? Guess where I am?

Maiyah: I don't know.

Nimco: WE ARE IN MADAGASCAR

Maiyah: Who is the girl with you? You had better not be with another girl.

Ali: Is my friend, don't be silly. Are you jealous?

Maiyah: No, no, no, I'm OK.

Nimco: We are going to a party and we're gonna find a girlfriend for Ali.

Maiyah hangs up the phone.

Ali: Why did you say that? I hate you.

Nimco: I love you too.

Animal man: You two are coming? The hike is about to start.

Nimco: Are you angry at me? We don't want to get left behind.

Ali: Let's go. I want to take some good pictures.

Animal man: There's some lemurs, look over there. Quick hide, if we don't scare them we can take a good picture.

They hide in a bush and Ali steps on a snake.

Ali: Ah ow ah ow, I've been bitten!

Nimco: Snake! Snake!

Animal man: Don't worry, I can get this snake! Leave it to me.

Animal man twists and fights with the snake.

Nimco: What kind of snake was it?

Animal man: It's a cobra. One of the danger snakes in the world.

Nimco: We need to call the hospital.

Animal man: No no is fine, we don't want to involve the hospital.

Nimco: We need to.

Ali: I need a doctor, I'm going to die and I'm dying.

In the hospital. Ali has gas to make him sleep.

Nimco: It's all your fault!

Animal man: I have to go now.

Nimco: I'm gonna find you.

Ali's girlfriend rings and Nimco picks it up.

Nimco: Hello Maiyah.

Maiyah: Who is that? Oh no not you again. What are you doing with my boyfriend's phone?

Nimco: Just listen. We need your help. Ali is hurt.

Maiyah: What did you do to my boyfriend?

Nimco: The snake has bitten him and he's ill.

Maiyah: If you need me I will get the next flight.

Doctor: He will be alright but he needs to take some tablets for the pain. You can go and see him.

Ali wakes up.

Ali: What is going on?

Scene seven

> Dear mother and father, I am writing to you from Afghanistan. It is cold and windy. We are happy. I feel happy because I went to the market and I bought a dress. Something happened the other day. I went to the desert and there was a sandstorm. It made me feel anxious. Hope to see you soon! Ali

Lesson plans and resources for EAL SoW

Lesson 1 (Page 96)

Resources

- Listening exercise and assessment form
- Pictures/images of journeys/transport scrolling through on IWB or stuck on walls (coloured A4 or A3 images). NB – These images should be linked to the verbs and adjectives used in the listening exercise.
- Key verbs from listening exercise displayed on the wall
- Large world map with stickers/pins to identify countries
- A box or suitcase of items and objects. Items inside the box/bag should link to the story in the listening exercise and journeys/travelling
- Paper plates or circular pieces of card – enough for one each

Lesson 2 (Page 102)

Resources

- Pictures/images and matching verbs, nouns and adjectives from last week stuck to the wall
- Genderless silhouette/figure to stick on world map
- Paper plate characters from last lesson

Lesson 3 (Page 103)

Resources

- Dictionaries and bilingual dictionaries where possible
- Computers with access to the internet

Lesson 4 (Page 104)

Resources

- World map
- Dictionaries and bilingual dictionaries where possible
- Postcard template (in resources)
- An empty, large picture frame, if possible. If not, a cardboard picture frame would suffice
- Digital camera
- Sticky notes
- Sign saying 'Question Wall' and designated space in room for where students can post sticky notes with thoughts, questions and queries about their learning

Lesson 5 (Page 106)

Resources

- Sticky notes of different colours
- Copies of Talk Booklet (in resources)
- Box with students' names on different slips of paper

Lesson 6 (Page 110)

Resources

- Listening exercise used in lesson 1
- World map with genderless silhouette/figure
- A different genderless silhouette/figure which is a different colour

EAL PLAYWRITING SCHEME OF WORK
Lesson 1: Journeys
PLTS: Creative Thinking; Self-Management; Teamwork

The TEEP Learning Cycle

1 Prepare for and Connect the Learning

Listening assessment takes place at the start of the session, explained to the students by their teacher (see example listening assessment in resources).

2 Agree Learning Objectives

Contextualise SoW, including concept of plays and playwriting. Elicit, where possible, whether students have been to the theatre or seen plays in different contexts/locations. Discuss what a character is and how you know.

- **Know** some verbs and adjectives linked to journeys and people
- **Apply** these verbs and adjectives to sentences about journeys and people
- **Describe** in more detail our own journey or another person's journey

3 Present New Information Through the Senses

Images of journeys/transport scrolling through on IWB or stuck on walls (coloured A4 or A3 images). *NB – These images should be linked to the verbs and adjectives used in the listening assessment.* The key words from the listening assessment (including nouns) should be on A4 sheets, stuck around the room. Students match the words to the pictures and, if possible, explain their choices with support from teacher/TA. Discuss. Encourage students to use words they know in English. TAs/teachers support.

Ask students about their journey to school.

How did they get to school? On a bus, in a car or walking? What did they do before that? Did they have breakfast? Did they play a computer game? Did they watch television? Who have they spoken to this morning before they got to school? Did anything happen on their journey to school?

Ask them to write three things down that they have done on their journey from bed to school, using a key verb from the listening assessment (these are also displayed on the wall). Model this first, using an example from the listening assessment.

4 Construct

Whole class discussion about journeys. What is a journey? What does this word mean? Refer to verbs on walls about travelling and journeys. Ensure you have images that relate to these words. World map displayed on wall. Students put stickers/pins on where they have travelled from and to, and attempt sentences to describe their journey using nouns, adjectives and verbs that they have learnt today. Students should be guided towards using the key words on the walls.

5 Apply to Demonstrate your New Understanding

This activity is about generating ideas about where the character in the listening assessment is going.

Have one box or suitcase of items and objects for the whole group, or give each small group a box/bag with a number of items to interrogate. *Items inside the box/bag should link to the story in the listening assessment and journeys/travelling,* for example a used train ticket. Pull items out of the box with the whole class, and question the class about this item and who it might belong to and why. For example, re the train ticket, "Where is this person travelling to? Why?" Alternatively, students could work in small groups creating thoughts, questions and ideas about the items and what they might reveal about the person who owns them. Adjust this according to the levels of English in the group. Refer to last learning objective – prompt students to describe this person in more detail using key words they have learnt this lesson. Students are supported by teaching assistants and EAL teachers/specialists. Teacher pulls ideas together as a whole group and records ideas on the board/IWB to be kept for future reference.

6 Review – step back and reflect on your learning

Explain to students that we have just thought of some ideas for a character. We're now going to think of some more ideas for characters, based on people we know.

Ask the group to reflect on someone they talked to on their journey to this country (refer back to the map of the world here). It might be someone they know, or someone who was a complete stranger. Perhaps that person didn't speak the same language as them. At this point you need to refer to the verb 'to talk' on a flashcard/card on wall. An image to go alongside this would also help EAL learners process what this means. Give students a paper plate/circular piece of card.

Pupils draw one person they talked to on their journey to this country, focusing on:

Their age
Their gender
What they looked like
Were they happy, sad etc.

Students write adjectives to describe the person on the plate, using the key words from the wall to help.

Ensure you emphasise that it is not the quality of the picture that matters; we're looking for what effective adjectives you can use to describe your person, who will become the basis for a character in a play. (Refer back to discussion about plays and characters earlier in lesson.)

Emphasise effective self-management skills and working to time to complete a task. New 'characters' are stuck on the wall – explain that these will form the basis for our character work next session.

Sample EAL listening exercise and assessment form

Simon lives with his mother and his older sister in a flat in Birmingham. He is 13 years old.

It is Saturday and Simon usually sleeps until 10 am at the weekend, but today his alarm wakes him up at 7.30 am.

He is angry to be woken up so early on a Saturday and he picks up his mobile phone to stop the alarm. He receives a text message from his friend Mohammed and he remembers that he must meet him at the train station at 8.30 am for their special trip.

Simon gets out of bed and goes to the kitchen to get a drink. He is thirsty and goes to the fridge for some orange juice. There isn't any orange juice and he can only find lemonade.

He goes to the bathroom and takes a shower. He brushes his teeth and then gets dressed. He can't find his favourite red T-shirt, so he has to wear his dirty sweater.

There is a noise from the other bedroom and he is worried that his mother will wake up. This is a secret trip and he needs to meet Mohammed before his mum and sister wake up.

He is hungry but he is late. He doesn't have time for breakfast because the bus leaves in ten minutes.

As he leaves the house, his sister Jane gets up and goes to the living room. She is wearing his favourite red T-shirt. Simon is very angry.

Simon runs for the bus but he still misses it. Mohammed will be worried if he is late. He goes back home to get his bicycle but he remembers that it is broken.

An aeroplane flies overhead and he wishes he could fly. He hears a train and realises he must run to the train station.

Finally he arrives at the train station and he runs to the ticket office to buy a return ticket to London. Mohammed sends him a text message from the platform.

Where r u Si?

Listening Exercise

NAME	
AGE	
FORM	
NATIONALITY	

Listen to the story and circle the correct answer.

Where does Simon live?

| House | Flat | Bungalow | Tent |

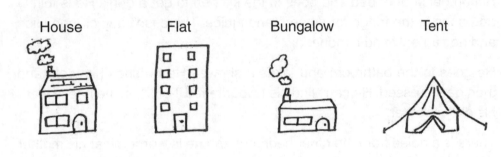

How old is Simon?

10 years old   15 years old   13 years old   16 years old

What wakes Simon up?

Alarm clock   Bird   Telephone   His mum

How does Simon feel to be woken up so early?

Happy Surprised Upset Angry

What does Simon drink?

Orange juice Lemonade Tea Coke

What colour is Simon's favourite T-shirt?

Blue Green Yellow Red

What is Simon worried about?

Waking up his mum Losing his red T-shirt Making noise

When does the bus leave?

Ten minutes	Ten hours	Ten seconds

Who is wearing Simon's red T-shirt?

Jane	John	Joanne	Jack

What does Simon go back home to get?

Bicycle	Bag	Skateboard	Trainers
		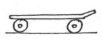	

What does Simon wish he could do?

Fly	Swim	Run	Hop

What does Simon hear?

Train	Aeroplane	Car	Bus

What does Simon buy at the train station?

Train ticket	Crisps	Drink	Newspaper

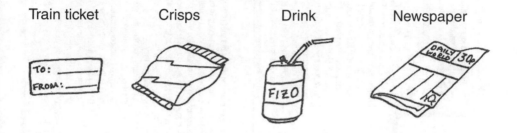

EAL PLAYWRITING SCHEME OF WORK

Lesson 2: Characters

PLTS: Creative Thinking; Teamwork

1 Prepare for and Connect the Learning

Pictures and matching verbs, nouns and adjectives from last week stuck to the wall. Students take it in turns to create a sentence about a journey. Model to the class first. For example:

I was worried I was going to miss my plane.
The bus ride was very long.

2 Agree Learning Objectives

- **Describe** a journey using nouns, verbs and adjectives
- **Explain** information about our characters
- **Understand** how to introduce a character to a scene

3 Present New Information Through the Senses

Refer to map of world from last lesson (this should be permanently displayed on the wall for the duration of the scheme of work). Students practise describing their own journeys again using nouns, verbs and adjectives. Where have we travelled from? How did we travel? Students put stickers/pins on map to show own journeys and describe them.

Reference first learning objective. Have we achieved it?

Stick a silhouette/shadow outline of a genderless character, on to the map. Who is this? Could this be our main character? What's their name? Where are they going in their bag? Where are they going? Where have they been? Where are they now? How do they feel? The group literally map out where this main character is going from country to country on the map – this provides the narrative structure for the play. Teacher records information about the main character and the list of countries the students identify. These will become the locations for the play. Students discuss. Record ideas on IWB.

The TEEP Learning Cycle

4 Construct

Paper plate 'characters' from last lesson should be stuck on the wall at the start of this lesson. Re-introduce them. These are some characters that we started thinking about last lesson. We're going to decide which ones are going to be in our own play and think about them in lots more detail. At this point also refer to the person on the world map that we have just thought about. The group should now decide on 8–10 characters for their play through discussion, presentation of different characters to the rest of the group etc. Teacher chooses most appropriate strategy for this.

Next, reference second learning objective. Each student chooses one character and explains more information about that character (these should preferably be typed up on an A3 document ready for the students to answer). Students should be able to take down the characters from the wall and have them on tables to refer to:

What is their name?
What did they have for breakfast?
Who do they live with?
Do they go to work?
Do they have a secret?
Do they have any brothers or sisters?
Do they have a mobile phone?
Do they have a hobby?
What's their favourite country?

How old are they?
Which country do they live in?
What are they wearing?
Do they go to school or college?
What is their favourite colour?
Do they live in a house, a flat, a caravan, a cave or a tent?
How much money do they have with them?
Where are they going today?
What did they do yesterday?

To include – actions too – what did they do earlier in the day, where were they yesterday etc. Share ideas with group.

6 Review – step back and reflect on your learning

Read scene.
What have we found out about our characters today?
How do they respond to other characters?
What are their likes and dislikes?
How did we introduce our characters to the scene?
What have we learnt today? How do we know?
Do we have a main character now? Who is he/she?

5 Apply to Demonstrate your New Understanding

Ref final learning objective – this is where we're going to do some writing. First of all, we're going to have a go together. We're going to carry on the story from the listening assessment where it finished last week – the story about Simon (see example listening assessment in resources). Then we're going to think about our own characters that we have developed, and write about them in the same story that will become our play. NB – we have included an example listening assessment that you could use. You could replace it with one of your own.

Read story from listening assessment again to pupils, without pausing. Get to where Simon meets Mohammed. How does Simon say hello to Mohammed? What does he say? How does he say hello? In what way? Is he happy, sad, angry, confused? Does he whisper, shout, pant? Why? As a group, write the first few lines of dialogue on the board. Model conventions of writing on board. Explain that this is part of a scene of our play. A scene is where something happens. This scene is set in the train station (it might be a different location if you use another listening assessment). Ask students to think about which of their own characters may be in this scene. What do they say to each other? What happens? Continue to write the scene as a whole group to build confidence and encourage oral rehearsal of vocabulary.

EAL PLAYWRITING SCHEME OF WORK

Lesson 3: Location

PLTS and Literacy: Creative Thinking;
Reflective Learning; Teamwork

---

1 Prepare for and Connect the Learning

Welcome. Revisit the scene the group wrote together last lesson. Check understanding of characters – who is the main character? What are his/her likes/dislikes? Where are they going? Why? Read as a group to reinforce understanding of new vocabulary and promote oral rehearsal of new vocabulary. Countries identified by group last lesson are listed on board or are written on large cards. Students identify where they are and stick them on the world map.

---

2 Agree Learning Objectives

- **Understand** what we mean by location and environment
- **Explain** how the location and environment affects the characters' journeys
- **Create** a scene in a specific location

---

3 Present New Information Through the Senses

Revisit map of world. What ideas did we have last lesson? Today we're learning about **location** and **environment**. What knows what these words mean? Opportunity to practise dictionary skills – more able English speakers and readers could look up 'location' and 'environment' and give group a definition of both (use bilingual dictionaries where possible to reinforce understanding. Ask students to identify what the location is in the group's first scene (e.g. a train station). Split the group in two. Ask one half to think what the train station (or another location) would be like at 9 a.m. (e.g. noisy, busy etc.). They should think of as many adjectives as they can to describe it. Ask the other half of the group to think of the same location at 11.30 p.m. or midnight (quiet, deserted etc.). They need to think of as many adjectives as they can to describe it. Time it – don't give them too long. Discuss. Make the link explicit to environment and how environment can change. Encourage pupils to think how environment can affect characters. Next, split the class into smaller groups and allocate each group a country that they identified last lesson. Each group researches ideas and information about that location. Groups have to come back with three key places/locations for each country, e.g. for the UK it might be London – Olympic village; Brick Lane; Cutty Sark. Each group feeds back. Whole group vote on one key location for each country. Each location could then become a scene that will be developed. NB – you can, of course, have as many countries as you like in the play but do note that it will take much longer to write the more countries you include. We recommend about four or five countries.

---

4 Construct

Explain that we will now focus on writing a scene in one of the locations that we have decided on. This scene is about our main character and what he/she does in this location. We are going to look at the first scene we wrote together last lesson. In what location is this set? Where are they? Our main character is going to come into this scene. Why is he/she at the station? (This is the location used in the listening assessment – see example in resources. You may want to choose a different listening assessment. This is fine, just have a definite location to refer to in the listening assessment – e.g. airport; bus station etc.) Where might he/she be going? Why? How would our main character behave in this location? Why? Link to second learning objective. As a group, continue to write the scene, incorporating the main character. Do not split into individual groups yet. Group writing increases confidence and enables oral rehearsal of new vocabulary before independent writing. Finish first scene.

---

6 Review – step back and reflect on your learning

Read first two scenes. What have we found out about our characters today? How do they respond to different locations? Why? What have we learnt today? How do we know? Encourage self-reflection and analysis of skills used.

The TEEP Learning Cycle

---

5 Apply to Demonstrate your New Understanding

Reference third learning objective. Explain that, as a group, we will now begin a scene two in one of our chosen locations from within the countries selected in lesson 1. Refer to shortlist of locations from earlier in the lesson. As a group, decide in which location this scene will be set. Then make the following decisions as a group:

- Which characters are in the scene? Refer to the paper plate characters that are stuck on the wall and decide.
- How are the characters connected/how do they know each other? Do they know the main character? How?
- What time of day is it in the scene? What else do we need to know about the environment? Is it noisy? Quiet? Busy?
- Who is already in the scene?

Regularly refer to key vocabulary

Write this scene as a group. Teachers use professional judgement to decide whether the group are able enough English users to split into smaller groups to write scenes in other locations with other characters. They may not be, and if not, just write this one scene as a whole group. In our experience, remaining as a whole group at this point works best.

EAL PLAYWRITING SCHEME OF WORK
Lesson 4: Location (2)
PLTS: Creative Thinking; Reflective Learning; Teamwork

1 Prepare for and Connect the Learning

Welcome. Revisit learning last lesson. What can you remember about the locations we researched? What is a location? What did we find out about our main character? Read scenes one and two.

2 Agree Learning Objectives

- **Understand** the difference between location and environment
- **Create** further scenes in specific locations
- **Analyse** the impact of the location and environment on the characters and their relationships with other characters

3 Present New Information Through the Senses

Ref first learning objective. Our focus again today is <u>location</u>. We need to make sure we understand what location is, and also what environment is. Dictionary race – look up and define location and environment. Students attempt to define both. Next, refer to research on countries from last lesson. Ask them, in their books/journals, to write down all the words they can for locations linked to the countries they had researched (e.g. Kabul, bazaars, river Nile etc.) and then to write down all the words they can think of linked to the environments of these locations (crowded, arid, hot etc.).

4 Construct

So what is the difference between location and environment? Reference first learning objective. Ensure that the students understand that environment – external conditions and surroundings' – is different from a location – e.g. a train station at 9 a.m. during rush hour is different from a train station at 11.30 p.m. – the location is the same but the environment is different and would impact on the way the characters behave.

Using the map, revisit the other countries from last lesson. Prompt students to recap on what decisions were made about location and environment. Explain that the students, in role as the main character, will write a postcard from their location explaining how the main character is feeling about the location and environment (remind them they will therefore be writing 'I am …', as the main character – but probably best not to say it is called 'first person' as this might be confusing). NB – you may need to explain what a postcard is and perhaps bring examples in from home. Split into groups and give them postcard templates (see resources). Less advanced English speakers and writers will need the more structured sentence stems; more advanced speakers won't. Differentiate and adapt the example template accordingly. Explain that the main character can be writing a postcard to anyone – family member, friend, colleague etc. Students decide who he/she is writing his/her postcard to and whether they're feeling happy, sad, worried etc. Listen to postcards. The postcards can function as monologue links between scenes when the whole play is written.

The TEEP Learning Cycle

6 Review – step back and reflect on your learning

Read scenes as a whole class. Establish Question Wall area of the room (you'll need a sign saying "Question Wall" and also different coloured sticky notes from those used earlier). What questions do we have about the scenes? What else do we want to know? Students can work in pairs to write down their questions on sticky notes and post on the wall. (You may need to model some questions first.) Questions to be kept and referred to next lesson to see whether we can answer them. What did we like about the scenes? Why?

5 Apply to Demonstrate your New Understanding

Ref first learning objective again, and also second learning objective. The last activity has helped us think about how our main character is feeling in certain locations. We're now going to create two more scenes for our play to explore in more detail how our main character responds to location and environment and how this affects his/her relationships with other people. Relate this back to the map activity in lesson 2 and how the main character is journeying from country to country? Where are they going? This must be reflected in the narrative of the play. Why is the character journeying from country to country? Where are they going? This must be reflected in the scenes to ensure continuity and action of journeys as a starting point for the scenes. Start writing the scenes for these two different locations as a whole group. Write the first four lines as a whole group for each scene, and then split the class into two separate groups to write the rest of the scene. This obviously depends on the size of your group. If you have a bigger group, split into smaller groups and give each group a location. Importantly, though, the scenes have to be begun as a whole class. Try to ensure groups are supported by a teacher/workshop leader and other adults including teaching assistants. By the end of the lesson you should have scenes three and four written.

Punctuate this activity with opportunities to reflect and analyse how the main character is feeling. Reference third learning objective. Explain that to 'analyse' means to look closely; to examine. Use this time for reflection as an opportunity to examine. Explain that to 'analyse' means to look closely; to examine. Use this time for reflection as an opportunity to begin to extend their English vocabulary. Use 'Who's in the Frame?' activity to do this: students decide how the main character is feeling at a particular point in the scene they're working on and explain why he/she is feeling like that. A student volunteers to be the main character and steps up to the front. He/she is handed an empty picture frame – they have to show the emotion the main character is feeling through their expression in the picture. Take photo (NB – check school permissions and protocol first). Check what the emotion is in English and students also write down what the emotion is in their home language. Do this a few times throughout the writing process and keep a record of what the emotions are in the different languages. Print out photos for next week and have emotions printed in different languages next lesson. Print out photos for next week and have emotions printed in different languages printed onto large laminated cards to label the 'Who's in the Frame?' pictures as the Prepare for Learning activity next lesson.

Dear........................,

I am writing to you from.......................

It is ....

....

....

I feel......................because........

....

....

Something happened the other day. I......

....

....

....

It made me feel.................................

Hope to see you soon!

Place Stamp Here

....

....

....

....

Place Stamp Here

....

....

....

....

EAL PLAYWRITING SCHEME OF WORK
Lesson 5: Deepening the Story
PLTS: Creative Thinking; Teamwork

1 Prepare for and Connect the Learning

Welcome. Revisit learning last lesson. Read scenes written last lesson so students get to hear the story as a whole. Have Question Wall area of the room established with a sign to indicate what it is.
Hand out two different coloured sticky notes. Ask students to:
Write one thing they know about the story
Write one thing they want to know about the characters (you will need to refer to these later in lesson)

2 Agree Learning Objectives

- **Analyse** the characters in more detail
- **Apply** our new ideas about our characters to our existing scenes to develop them further

3 Present New Information Through the Senses

Ref first learning objective – analysing our characters.
Explain that analyse means to look closely; to examine. We're going to deepen our understanding of our characters. Students work in pairs (pair less confident speakers with more confident, advanced speakers).
Hand out Talk Booklets (see resources).
Explain concept of what the Talk Booklet is and the rules (they are on the first page of the Talk Booklet).
Pairs choose one character each from any scene and work through statements and questions in Talk Booklets. Again, this promotes the oral rehearsal of English to promote confidence.

4 Construct

Reference learning objective again, or ideally ask students to reference the objective so they know themselves where they are in the progression of their learning. Around the room have large outlines of characters with their names above them, in a Role on the Wall style.
Explain that the outlines of figures are the characters from our play. Hand out larger-sized sticky notes.
Ask pairs to write down on the sticky notes what they found out about their characters from their Talk Booklet conversations and stick on the figures.
They can work in their pairs to do this. Once these are stuck on the outlines of characters you have a 'gallery' where students read contributions from other students.

The TEEP Learning Cycle

5 Apply to Demonstrate your New Understanding

Explain how we have managed to deepen our understanding of some of our characters.
Now we need to apply these ideas to the scenes that we wrote last lesson.
As a whole group, revisit and develop scenes three and four, applying the ideas they have explored about their characters earlier in the lesson.
Read developed scenes.

6 Review – step back and reflect on your learning

Read play so far. Repeat exercise from earlier – get them to think about one thing they want to know about the story and characters. Explain to them that you expect everyone to contribute thoughts and ideas. This time, students don't write it down but have Think Time (at least two minutes) to think about what their ideas are. Have a box with all students' names on slips of paper. Pull names out of the box. (Alternatively use one of the many programs on IWBs that select names for you.) That student has to say what they want to know about the story or characters/a specific character. You may not have time to get around everyone but it's a good activity for getting everyone ready to contribute and for setting up expectations that everyone will participate.

Playwriting Talk Booklet

Instructions to accompany the Talk Booklet.
Step 1: Work with a partner — A & B
Step 2: A will be the Questioner, B the Respondent
Step 3: The conversation will proceed as follows:

A — Questioner
Ask a question. Take only one question at a time. After asking a question, pause to offer your partner time to think about a response.

After your partner responds, take time to reflect. Pause, giving yourself and your partner time to think.

Occasionally, after two or three responses, or more frequently if appropriate, summarise the latest response with a paraphrase but don't offer your own opinion. Alternatively, probe for clarification by saying, "Tell me more about…".

If you feel uncomfortable about asking a question, rephrase it or skip it.

B — Respondent
When answering a question from your partner, respond at any level of disclosure with which you are comfortable. If at any time you choose not to respond to a particular question just say, "I pass." No reasons for passing are necessary.

Choose one of the characters from any of the scenes. Describe three things about them.

Describe something that happened to your chosen character last week.

Explain your chosen character's objective.
What is it?
Why?

Explain one thing that your character really wants in life and why it's important to them.

EAL PLAYWRITING SCHEME OF WORK
Lesson 6: The End of the Journey
PLTS: Creative Thinking; Reflective Learning; Teamwork

1 Prepare for and Connect the Learning

NB – depending on the time you have available and the size of your group, you may want to split this lesson over two lessons. The flexibility of the TEEP cycle enables you to do this quite easily.

Welcome. Revisit learning last lesson. Outline what we want to achieve by the end of the lesson – a finished play written by everyone and a completed listening assessment.

2 Agree Learning Objectives

- **Create** further scenes in different locations
- **Apply** ideas about character and location to these scenes
- **Evaluate** what we have learnt and how we have learnt

3 Present New Information Through the Senses

Read scenes written last lesson again so students get to hear the story as a whole.

4 Construct

Reference first learning objective and what we want to achieve by the end of the session today.
Explain how we have managed to deepen our understanding of some of our characters last lesson.
We're now going to create some new scenes in different groups in those locations that are still on our list.
Split into smaller groups to write scenes in different locations.
Teachers and teaching assistants support groups.
Come together as a whole group.
Read new scenes.
Write final scene for the play as a whole group.
Read.
Re-read the postcards written earlier in the scheme of work.
Decide where they will be inserted into the play – perhaps as structural devices to link scenes.

The TEEP Learning Cycle

6 Review – step back and reflect on your learning

Revisit the world map on wall and the figure of main character, stuck to the map. Where has he/she been in the world? What has he/she learnt – about different countries, about other people, and about himself/herself?
Introduce a different outline of a 'figure' on the map (it could be a different colour or shape to show it's a different person). Explain to the group that this person represents each one of us. What have we learnt? What do we know about different countries now? What do we know now that we didn't know at the start of the project? What skills have we developed? How have we developed these skills? What skills have we worked together as a team? Have we used our listening skills? Have we used our creative thinking skills? How? Students come up to the front to move the figure of themselves on the map and explain their ideas, in full sentences.

5 Apply to Demonstrate your New Understanding

Reintroduce listening assessment from first lesson in this scheme of work. Be very clear about explaining how it's assessing listening skills, not writing skills. Explain that we're going to see whether they have improved their listening and understanding of different English words in the story. Students undertake listening assessment.

Citizenship and Community SoW

Introduction to Citizenship and Community SoW

This SoW has been designed to bring students together to focus on elements of Citizenship and community at all levels: in school, in their local communities and home towns, cities or villages and on an international level. The process of this group play could work in many different ways within school and at any key stage. It could also work with mixed-age or mixed-ability groups. Some suggested ideas for using this SoW to support the exploration and discussion of ideas around community and Citizenship would be:

- Incorporating it into Citizenship days or focus weeks for KS3, KS4 or KS5. Many UK state schools incorporate the teaching of Citizenship into a number of themed whole days across the academic year where the usual curriculum is collapsed and only Citizenship is taught. Other schools have Citizenship focus weeks where a Citizenship theme is taught across the course of the week in all subject areas.
- Developing it into a transitional project for year 5 and 6 students from feeder primary schools working with current year 7 or older students.
- A transitional project for prospective AS/A2 level sociology, history, geography or English students moving from KS4 to KS5 to inspire them and explore issues and ideas prevalent in their new courses.

- A family learning community project where students and their families explore issues that affect their local communities. This SoW offers the opportunity for different generations to work together, enriching each other's understanding of what is a pertinent issue for them and how different members of the community behave and are treated.
- A cross-curricular project where teachers from different curriculum areas collaborate to plan a project on a specific theme based on community – e.g. Black History Month; carnival; the school's chosen charity; slavery; the Holocaust etc. The development of the play is a culmination of the same theme explored in all subject areas. Initial research around events and incidents that have affected the communities and/or periods of history students are focusing on will need to be done or incorporated into the lesson plans.

There is flexibility around the timings of these sessions due to the versatility of the SoW and how it can be adapted for various groups. The versatile nature of the TEEP cycle enables teachers to teach the different phases of the cycle across a longer period of time as well as in a one-hour or 70-minute lesson. Thus these lessons, or "sessions" as we have called them due to the flexible nature of this SoW, can be delivered over a period of time that is best suited to the needs of the group and the required outcomes for the group or school.

This SoW has been designed with an incident that affects a community as the premise for the play and project as a whole. The incident must be something that has happened in the past, be it the immediate past or a moment in history that has affected a wider community as well as the immediate characters, and should raise themes that impact upon society as a whole. We recommend using a real incident that a lot of the students within the group would be aware of. Local newspapers are a great source for stimuli for community stories and research into certain periods of history. A project, for example, to celebrate the anniversary of the Battle of Britain would involve more preparation beforehand. If you are dealing with a larger event or period in history of such national and international significance, the research should be focused upon finding out the more local stories, for example how the bombing of a school in Coventry affected the school children in the 1940s. The play could begin the morning after the bombing took place and the children can't find their school. *One Night in November* by Alan Pollock, published by Josef Weinberger Plays and produced three times by the Belgrade Theatre, Coventry is a play set around and on the night of the Coventry bombings and could also be used as resource material.

The incident needs to be a defined event that has happened within a community, and the characters in the play will be dealing with the consequences of this event and how it has changed and does change their lives during the course of the drama they are writing. Examples of such events are:

1. A new zoo has opened in the middle of a quiet village
2. A flood has devastated a village in Pakistan
3. A farmer has been told that he can't sell his meat any more because his cows are descendants of clones
4. All people suffering from leprosy in Greece are ordered to live on a tiny island, Spinalonga, off the coast of Crete
5. A village has a wind farm erected one mile away
6. The Pope has visited the Oratory Church in Edgbaston, Birmingham.

It is useful to refer to recent events for which students will have some reference in the examples or that they have prior understanding of and have researched in, for example, history, science, geography or English lessons.

Examples of texts to use

Ostrich Boys, adapted by Carl Miller from the novel by Keith Gray, is published by Methuen and could be used as a play exploring an incident that has impacted upon a group of boys, their family and the school community. Blake has gone into the home of their deceased friend Ross in order to steal the urn with his ashes inside. His friends want to take him on a trip to his namesake place Ross in Scotland. The play follows their journey to Ross with Ross's ashes and their adventures along the way, and the realisation towards the end that he might have committed suicide and not been accidentally knocked down by a car.

Another play that could be used here is *The Day the Waters Came* by Lisa Evans, published by Oberon and produced by Theatre Centre. This play explores how Hurricane Katrina devastated and fragmented communities in New Orleans in 2005. The extracts from *Kingswood News*, written by students from St Alban's Academy, Birmingham, could also be used in lesson 1. If you are using this as a transitional project for Year 6 and 7 students, *Of the Terrifying Events on the Hamelin Estate* by Philip Osment, published by Oberon in the *Class Acts* trilogy in the reading list, is aimed at Year 6 students and explores the estate's response to the invasion of rats.

In lesson 2, phase 3, it is worth pushing the students to think outside of their obvious choices for locations and to include both public and private spaces. This will allow characters to come together in the public spaces who wouldn't normally meet, offering potential for rich and unexpected outcomes. The private places should be mixed too, because what one character may think of as a private space (a living room) might feel very exposed to another.

In lesson 3, phase 4, the structuring of the play in relation to when the incident happened pushes students to think about the consequences of events and actions. It explores the notion that each scene is a complete unit of action in itself that pushes the narrative forward, yet is connected to what has happened immediately before it. In a transitional project with Year 6 and Year 7 from Hawbush Primary and Wordsley Secondary schools in Walsall, West Midlands, a Year 6 student stated: 'It's the incident, solution and end of investigation,' seeming to have inherently understood the reactive nature of characters and events in live drama and emulating a three-act structure.

We would advise pushing the incidents that come up as a group into having an element of ambiguity about them. This stops an immediate 'start, middle and end' scenario, which can result in some students saying what is right and what is wrong, hence detracting from the aim of this as a project to allow multiple voices to be heard through this active collaboration. The process should promote empathy and the necessity to listen to all points of view. The use of an incident that has affected a community should encourage thinking about consequences and how things are connected, even if they don't appear so on the surface – how something that happens in one area of the world or within a community can affect many people, if not millions, in different ways.

Case study

A group of Year 7 students at St Alban's Academy, Birmingham developed *Kingswood News*, a play using a similar SoW, in 2007/8 when the story of the disappearance of Madeleine McCann was still very present across the media. The project was led by Clare Lovell, Literary Assistant at Birmingham Repertory Theatre. This was an event that resonated with the group and they decided to develop a play around the disappearance of a child; the play explored the community after this had happened. The child in the play was at secondary school and the characters were her immediate school friends and family, through to the police and the local shopkeepers. The play retained a sense of ambiguity at the end, which enabled multiple voices through the various characters to explore the themes of a community trying to deal with such an upsetting event. This lack of solution made the narrative more complex and enabled more dramatic action and subsequently subtext.

We have included two extracts from *Kingswood News* to demonstrate the multiplicity of voices that can be heard through its numerous characters and their different relationships to each other and the event. This variety of characters results in a complexity of emotions and responses from various members of one community. The first extract illustrates the impact on parents, who are now reluctant to let their children out because of the recent disappearance of Penny. It also introduces rumour and blame, which are often rife and active emotions after an event that has shaken a community out of its status quo. Aunt Mary's arrival introduces another voice to the domestic argument by accusing 'that grumpy old man', increasing the threat that the outside world now has on the inside worlds of its community members.

The second extract in the salon demonstrates the importance of illustrating a number of characters who will be affected by the event to varying degrees. The way in which the rumour, almost like a baton, is passed on from one character to another, keeps the story alive in their minds and pushes the narrative forward.

Kingswood News by Year 7 pupils, St Alban's Academy, 2007/8

The following extracts are examples of how the disappearance of Penny, the paper girl in their play, was starting to affect the wider community.

Teenage sisters Michelle and Marisha are arguing.

Michelle: That's it! I'm going out!

Sarah: No, you're not, young lady. Haven't you heard about the kidnapping?

Michelle: So? I don't care.

Marisha: You should. That might be you next. Ooh!

Michelle: Shut up!

Sarah: Girls! Leave each other alone. You won't be going anywhere, either of you.

Michelle: Why, Mom? It's not fair.

Marisha: Shut up, you. Baby! Drama queen!

Sarah: Anyway, I'm going out soon. Aunt Mary will be here in about 2 minutes.

Exit Sarah. Enter Mary.

Mary: Hello Girls.

Michelle and Marisha: Hi Aunty.

Mary: Have you heard about this abduction? They say the girl was taken on her way to her before school job. How sad.

Michelle: I know. It's because of her that I can't go out.

Mary: I think it's that grumpy old man, he is so much happier now she's gone.

Michelle: I was always curious about that man. He looked at me in this way that I didn't really like.

Marisha: How do you know? You can't just blame someone. Imagine if that was you, what would you say?

Michelle: Ok, why are you sticking up for him against me!

Mary: Ok girls what do you want to do? You have a choice between a game of chess or twister.

Michelle: I want to play twister, its sick!

Mary: I'm going to get the game. One second.

She leaves.

Marisha: I've got a better game. Let's escape out the house, it will be fun. Promise you won't tell.

Michelle: Okay, as long as you take the blame, I'll go.

Marisha: No-one's going to take the blame. Quickly, she's coming.

Michelle and Marisha go out of the house. Aunt Mary comes down with the twister mat and can't find the girls.

Mary: Girls? Where are you? This isn't funny.

This extract is halfway into a scene where Lucy has popped out of the salon to get some sugar.

Outside Lucy has bumped into Sarah in the street

Sarah: Have you heard about the kidnapping of the paper girl?

Lucy: You're joking aren't you?

Sarah: No. She hasn't been in school and she didn't deliver all of her round today. Her mom has reported her missing.

Lucy: I better get back to the salon and tell the others.

Sarah: I hope she's ok.

Lucy: Yeah, so do I. Okay bye.

Lucy arrives back at the salon.

Stacey: You've been quick. Where's the sugar?

Lucy: I know why we didn't get the paper today!

Stacey: Why?

Lucy: Because the papergirl went missing earlier.

Stacey: Oh my gosh, really?

Lucy: Yeah, I just saw Sarah and she told me that she wasn't in school and she didn't finish off her paper round. Her mom has reported her missing.

Stacey shouts into the kitchen.

Stacey: Char, have you heard this? That girl went missing!

Charlotte: What girl?

Stacey: The paper girl.

Charlotte: Oh you're joking aren't you? This world is getting worse.

Louise: Oh I feel bad now for going off on one about my paper.

Lucy: It's alright, you didn't know, did you?

Louise: Yeah.

Stacey finishes Louise's hair.

Louise: Aw, it looks beautiful, thanks a bunch.

Stacey: That's £15 please.

Louise: Here you go, have a tip since you tried so hard on it.

Stacey: That's really generous of you, really it's nothing.

Charlotte: Poor girl, that Penny. We're going on like nothing's happened, I hope she's alright. *Her voice drifts away.*

Louise: *sadly* I don't know what I would do if it was my child.

Lesson plans and resources for Citizenship and Community SoW

Lesson 1 (Page 122)

Resources

- Video/images of a flowing river
- Sticky notes
- Blank incident/event graphic organiser (in resources)
- Digital camera

Lesson 2 (Page 124)

Resources

- Sticky notes
- Dictionaries
- Large sheets of paper
- Character History Sheet (see Core SoW resources lesson 4)
- Sign saying 'Question Wall' and designated space in room for where students can post sticky notes with thoughts, questions and queries about their learning

Lesson 3 (Page 125)
Resources

- Sticky notes
- Character History Sheets from last lesson
- Large outlines of characters drawn onto large sheets of paper
- Washing line/string
- Different sized pieces of paper or card 'pegged' up on the line (alternatively you could have real items of clothing on the line!)
- Question Box or Question Wall

Lesson 4 (Page 126)
Resources

- 'Washing line' from last lesson
- Large outlines of characters drawn onto large sheets of paper from last lesson
- Talk Booklet (see EAL SoW resources, lesson 5)

Lesson 5 (Page 127)
Resources

- 'Washing line' from previous two lessons
- Plain A3 paper
- Sticky notes

CITIZENSHIP AND COMMUNITY PLAYWRITING
SCHEME OF WORK
Session 1: Memories
PLTS: Teamwork and Creative Thinking

The TEEP Learning Cycle

1 Prepare for and Connect the Learning

Big picture of project shared with the group about writing a play together that focuses on issues that affect a community – either our own community or one that we have researched.

2 Agree Learning Objectives

- **Identify** some memories to act as a focus for our play
- **Apply** these ideas to the planning of our play
- Begin to **describe** in more detail the main incident and characters involved in our play

3 Present New Information Through the Senses

Reference first learning objective. Students walk around the space. Explain to them you want them to think about their life, the whole of it, like a river running past (you might want to have a video/images of a flowing river on your IWB to help students imagine this). Allow memories to flow past. Find something you remember that is of interest – an event, a moment, an image – and explore it. Students write down memory on a sticky note – it could be one word, a few words, or a sentence.

Students start walking again. Allow the 'river' to start flowing again, letting the memory they have written slide away. Students think of their life last year as if it were a video. They find something of interest, something that was important or significant, and replay the scene over a few times. Summarise it in a few words or a line and write it down on a sticky note and stick on the wall.

NB – do the following three points if you have time/gauge the group and see how they are coping with it:

Students now think of their life this year and repeat the process

They think of their life last week and repeat the process

Students look at everything they have written and find three or four questions the words or phrases prompt, and write them down.

4 Construct

We are still focusing on the first learning objective, as a starting point for our play. Ask students to walk around the space again. Students go and look at the first memory they wrote down and stuck on the wall. Students say the memory to themselves, a chair, a window, the wall or any other object in the room. Students pair up. Each partner tells their partner their memory. Each partner repeats it and learns it. Swap memories. Forget your own memory, you have given it away. Everyone now joins a circle – either sitting on the floor or on chairs. Close eyes. Everyone has someone else's memory. Students tell the group as much of the memory as they can. Explain they won't hold all the memories in their minds – just fragments and images that have stayed with them. This is fine.

Students now work on their own, writing down as much as they can remember from what's been said – words, images, phrases, scraps of information. Begin with 'I remember …'. Feed back to partner or group. What images stand out most? Why?

5 Apply to Demonstrate your New Understanding

Explain to the students that we are now going to use our memories to think of an event, an incident from which our whole play will emanate.

Give each student a sticky note. Ask them to think of and write down a local memory for the students – an incident that has actually happened and is shared by quite a lot of people in their community, in their street, in their schools etc. Please see the preamble for examples. The incident could have ramifications in the wider world (e.g. the floods in Pakistan) and how it affects the immediate community and then families in the UK. Additionally, the incident does not have to be a memory shared by the students themselves, it could also be an incident that the group have researched in other lessons – for example in history, geography, science, English, RE etc. It could even be an incident in the past that has happened to the local community that students have researched as part of a local history project. Students pair up and share ideas. Stick ideas for incidents/events on walls.

Students share memories of incidents in the group. Teacher/workshop leader lists ideas on the IWB and questions class about who is affected by the incident. Encourage students to think as widely as possible. Students decide as a group on the most striking/memorable memory of an incident. This will be the incident at the centre of the play.

Reference second learning objective. Whole-group planning. Blank graphic organiser of incident on IWB (see resources). Students provided with copies on A4 or A3. Whole-class planning of ideas: 'what is the incident? Who is the incident? Who is immediately affected by the incident? Who next?' until full plan of ideas for play is pulled together.

6 Review – step back and reflect on your learning

Reference third learning objective. What further ideas do we have about our play and our characters?

Students walk around the room, looking at the memories that were stuck on the walls earlier. Use these as a basis for generating further ideas about characters and the main incident. Students share ideas with whole group and record them on different-coloured sticky notes and stick them at the front of the room, or write ideas on the IWB. Volunteers share ideas. Teacher collects these ideas (if possible take photos of these sticky notes) to use as the starting point for a Prepare for Learning activity next session.

Graphic Organiser
Who does the incident affect?

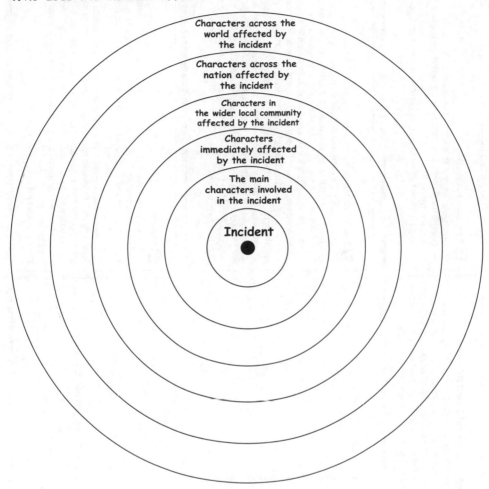

Characters across the
world affected by
the incident

Characters across the
nation affected by
the incident

Characters in
the wider local community
affected by the incident

Characters
immediately affected
by the incident

The main
characters involved
in the incident

Incident

CITIZENSHIP AND COMMUNITY PLAYWRITING
SCHEME OF WORK
Session 2: Location and characters
PLTS: Teamwork and Creative Thinking

1 Prepare for and Connect the Learning

Welcome. "Big picture" for project shared again. Any questions from last week? Photos of sticky notes from last session's Review scrolling through on IWB for all students to read. Discussion about further ideas for characters based on the sticky notes from last week's Review activity.

2 Agree Learning Objectives

- **Identify** what we mean by location and environment
- **Describe** the different locations in the play and **explain** how location might affect characters and our story
- **Create** character histories for our emergent characters and begin to develop our ideas in detail

3 Present New Information Through the Senses

Reference first learning objective. Can we define what we mean by location and environment? Think, pair, share – think on own first (and attempt to write definition), pair up to refine definition (use dictionaries if necessary) and then share with whole group. What's the difference? Revisit planning from last session about the incident for the play. Where would our first location for the play be? Decide as a group. Have a large sheet of paper in the middle of the space with the name of the first location of the play (e.g .park, high street, post office etc.). Ref second learning objective. This is our first location. What's in it? Students, in pairs, write their ideas on sticky notes and stick on the paper. Discuss. Place other labelled pieces of paper around the space that represent other locations of the world of the play. Create the world of the play on the floor. Reference second learning objective. Students think about the buildings and what they are like. Annotate 'buildings' with sticky notes with ideas about what might be in them, as before.

The TEEP
Learning
Cycle

4 Construct

Now we're going to think about the characters who are in the different locations and create a maximum of 12 characters. Use the locations to decide who will be in the play. Students record ideas on sticky notes and place on the locations, exploring the 'world' of the play as they go.

Whole-group discussion – use cardboard-cutout people to symbolise characters in the play (ideally they would be freestanding if possible, so they can be moved around the room) to start to think about where these characters go and how and why they move from location to location. For example, an old man might only walk from his house on the estate to the shops and back home because he can't walk very far. Students think about how location affects character and explain.
Revisit and refine list of 12 (or fewer) characters.

6 Review – step back and reflect on your learning

Check progress.
Revisit learning objectives.
What have we learnt?
What have we achieved?
How do we know?
Have a space in the room allocated as a Question Wall or instead have a Question Box. Both need to be labelled as such to make them 'special' and focus attention.
Students write down any further questions, thoughts or comments they have about the location, characters or incident that they would like to explore next lesson.

5 Apply to Demonstrate your New Understanding

Reference third learning objective.
Students in pairs.
Allocate each pair one character.
The pair jointly develop a character history for that character, exploring ideas (see Core SoW resources).

Group discussion and feedback to rest of group.

CITIZENSHIP AND COMMUNITY PLAYWRITING
SCHEME OF WORK
Session 3: Mapping the Play
PLTS: Teamwork and Creative Thinking

The TEEP Learning Cycle

1 Prepare for and Connect the Learning

Welcome. Any questions from last week? Students write down any further questions, thoughts or comments they have about the location, characters or incidents from last lesson and stick them on the Question Wall or put them in the Question Box. Discuss.

2 Agree Learning Objectives

- **Identify** what events will happen in our play and **explain** how the different locations and characters affect/contribute to the events that happen
- **Understand** how to begin a scene and engage the audience through conflict
- **Apply** this new understanding to writing a scene(s)

3 Present New Information Through the Senses

Explain to the pupils that in order to achieve our first learning objective we need to ensure we fully understand the 'back stories' for our characters. Students post up character history sheets on walls as a 'gallery'. Stick on the wall large different outlines/silhouettes of our characters, similar to a Role on the Wall outline that you might use in drama or English lessons. Ask students to synthesise what they have found out by reading the character histories and think of a number of adjectives to describe these different characters. Either write the adjectives directly onto the character outlines or write onto sticky notes. Discuss as a class. Who are these people? How are they connected?

4 Construct

Having made notes and understood the characters in more detail, the students now need, as a group, to map out the events for the play. Reference first learning objective. The incident they have identified has already happened before the play begins; but when in the past did it happen? Has it happened in the last minute? Yesterday? Two years ago? For example, if the students were writing a play about the 2010 floods in Pakistan the play might begin with the floods having started in the last hour and then the characters in the play will start to deal with the immediate emergency and the news breaking worldwide.

Next, have a literal 'washing line' strung up across the space with different-sized pieces of card/paper 'pegged' (paperclipped) on it. Explain that each item on the washing line represents scenes in the play. This activity is about the story and timeframe of the play. The group need to decide and explain:

   When the scene takes place in relation to the incident
   Where the scene takes place – is it a big or small scene in terms of what happens?
   What happens in the scene – refer back to all the locations
   Who is in the scene.

For example, taking the 2010 Pakistan floods as a starting point for a play, the first scene may be in Pakistan as it happens; the second scene could be someone watching the news in the UK who has a relative in Pakistan; the third and/or subsequent scenes could be about that person trying to get help to his/her relatives and so on.

Write this information on the washing line 'items' (ask another teacher to do this for you) and 'peg' up. What does our washing-line narrative for the play look like now? What happens?

5 Apply to Demonstrate your New Understanding

We've done a lot of work on thinking about our characters and mapping out the story and timeframe of the play. Now we're going to take what we have learned about our characters and play and apply it to writing a scene, learning about how to engage an audience through conflict.

Reference second and third learning objectives – we're going to understand how to begin a scene and engage the audience through conflict.

Ask the group for different ways of greeting people and write their suggestions on the board. Do not change the spelling of their suggestions and ask for the way they would spell these greetings. They should be different ways of saying hello and get them to think about how they greet different people – e.g. how they greet a friend; how they greet a teacher; how they greet a parent and how they greet a stranger. Give a few examples:

Hello; Hi; Safe etc. List on board.

Ask the group for different ways of saying 'I don't want to talk to you.' Again ask the group to consider how they say this to a stranger, parent, sibling, friend etc. and give a few examples. List their ideas on the board, e.g.:

Sorry, I've got to catch the bus; Leave me alone; Whatever; Laters etc.

Reference characters and timeframe of play. Decide which two characters will be in the first scene. How might one of the characters greet the other character? Ask the group to choose one of the greetings. This will be the first line of their play and will be the first line for 'A' (or whatever the name of the character is). Write this on the board so that they can see the layout:

E.g. A: Hi

Now ask the group to choose one from the other list and this will be the first line for 'B'.

E.g. B: Leave me alone.

These will be the first two lines of the scene:

E.g. A: Hi

A: Hi
B: Leave me alone.

Ask pupils for a suggestion for the next line for A:

A: Hi
B: Leave me alone.
A: *new line from students*

Continue writing scene together. Consider location and environment and status of characters and how this impacts/affects the conflict in the scene.

Get students to summarise how they were able to do this and how conflict is demonstrated. What engages the audience? Why?

6 Review – step back and reflect on your learning

Read the opening scene. Questions, thoughts, comments, observations? Reflection/Think Time – stick questions on Question Wall.

CITIZENSHIP AND COMMUNITY PLAYWRITING
SCHEME OF WORK
Session 4: Play structure and timeframe
PLTS: Teamwork; Creative Thinking;
Reflective Learning

1 Prepare for and Connect the Learning

Welcome.

Play 'washing line' strung up in room as pupils enter.

Students invited to read washing line to re-familiarise themselves with the story.

2 Agree Learning Objectives

- **Evaluate** the structure and timeframe of our play
- **Apply** this understanding to creating further scenes
- **Evaluate** how our characters have changed at the end of our scenes

3 Present New Information Through the Senses

Reference first learning objective and washing line.

Is every scene necessary?

Is there a complete story?

Group decide which scenes stay and which need to go.

Draw out that what happens at the end of the play and each scene is a small unit of action along the way to get to this point.

Ask group how each character will have changed by the end of the play.

Record this in large letters on each character outline (that should still be stuck on walls around the space).

4 Construct

Reference first learning objective again.

We've evaluated the structure, but what about the timeframe?

Group agrees whether the play happens over two hours, two days, two weeks, two years etc. The timeframe doesn't have to be linear but could go backwards or forwards in time. There is no need for chronology unless the group decides that is how they want the play to unfold.

Agree on scenes and split group into pairs. Allocate scenes to pairs.

Before they write their scenes, distribute Talk Booklets to help them construct and focus their ideas.

The TEEP Learning Cycle

6 Review – step back and reflect on your learning

After the scenes have been written, pairs read their scenes and decide what has changed for each character by the end of the scene. If nothing has changed for the characters, they will need to think about how they could develop their scene further.

Each character needs to have changed in some way by the end of each scene – it can be a small change but there needs to be a change.

Read scenes as a whole group if time.

5 Apply to Demonstrate your New Understanding

Reference second learning objective.

Write the scenes in their pairs.

CITIZENSHIP AND COMMUNITY PLAYWRITING
SCHEME OF WORK
Session 5: Final workshop
PLTS: Teamwork; Creative Thinking;
Reflective Learning

1 Prepare for and Connect the Learning

Welcome.

Play 'washing line' strung up in room as pupils enter.

Students invited to read washing line to re-familiarise themselves with the story.

2 Agree Learning Objectives

- **Evaluate** our scenes
- **Reflect** on our scenes and the questions from our peers
- **Apply** any changes to our scenes based on our evaluation and reflection

3 Present New Information Through the Senses

Reference first learning objective and washing line.

Explain process for today and how the writers will need to cast their scenes from students amongst the group; students will be actors as well as writers today. All students, including those watching, will ask questions of the writer about their scene.

4 Construct

Reference first learning objective.

Stuck on wall have plain A3 sheets with scene 1, scene 2, scene 3 etc written at the top of each of them (so you need as many sheets as there are scenes).

As each scene is acted out, students state and ask the writers the following (but the writers do not answer the questions; they write them in their notebooks):

One thing they liked about the scene

A question about the scene – this can be about a character or anything else that came to mind

Something that interests them about the scene

Students also write their question about the scene on a sticky note and stick onto the relevant Scene Question Sheet on the wall for future reference for the writers.

The TEEP Learning Cycle

6 Review – step back and reflect on your learning

Writers now read the whole play, or alternatively other students join the group to read the play as actors. Writers become the audience as well as the writers.

Discuss play. Reflect on and celebrate success.

NB – you may need one more session to refine the scenes after this workshop session, as the writers may need more time to respond to and develop their scenes after the comments and questions.

5 Apply to Demonstrate your New Understanding

Reference second learning objective.

Once all of the scenes have been performed, look at the washing line again.

Is the play complete or are there scenes missing?

If there is a scene missing, write it as a group.

Writers then go back and make any changes to their scenes as a response to the questions and after listening to the overall play.

Writers reference Scene Question Sheets on walls.

6

Personal, Social and Health Education (PSHE) SoW

Introduction to PSHE SoW

This SoW has been developed with PSHE – Personal Social and Health Education – and aspects of emotional literacy in mind. Based around the idea of 'secrets', it is therefore open-ended enough for schools to develop it to apply to any year group, or indeed mixed-age or mixed-ability group at KS3. It could be used to explore coping with feelings/anger management, sex or drugs education, eating disorders, starting at a new school or other PSHE themes.

We have developed the SoW as a 'Play in a Day' model, where the students work together to write a group play over the course of a school day. Many UK schools are teaching aspects of PSHE or Citizenship through themed days, where the usual curriculum is suspended and the students focus on a specific PSHE theme. This SoW therefore enables a unique way of exploring aspects of PSHE through student collaboration in writing a whole play in a day.

The SoW demonstrates the versatility of the TEEP cycle and demonstrates how it can be taught over the course of a day, as well as in an hour or 70-minute lesson. We have outlined approximate timings for the day, based on a usual school day of around five one-hour lessons, but this is of course adaptable to the school. There is an overview of the whole day on a lesson plan, and a more detailed explanation of the day and each session. This was to explicate some of the ideas in more detail for the teachers involved, some of whom may have no experience whatsoever of teaching playwriting and may be teachers of PSHE or other subjects. It guides the teacher through, step by step, so each phase of the day is clear.

Examples of texts to use

The SoW has been designed with the idea of secrets at its core, the idea prompted by Fin Kennedy's play *Stolen Secrets* (see Core SoW resources). This play began its life with the exercise of boxes being placed around the school where people would put in their secrets, which later became the basis for the play's narrative. In this SoW, students read an extract from 'Make 'n' Mend' from *Stolen Secrets* and explore this idea in detail, considering their own characters and what secrets they possess, and how their characters might react in different locations and situations. This enables the students to think clearly about coping with feelings and emotions, and allows them to consider how to respond to a situation by depersonalising it; it is the character, rather than themselves, in the situation.

Case study

A group of Year 7 students at Pittville School, Cheltenham, developed a play over the course of a day focusing on 'Dealing with Feelings' as part of PSHE. The play was set in a school, and different characters emerged over the course of the morning, all with very different secrets. The play enabled the students to explore the characters' feelings and create ways in which the characters could cope with these feelings. If the characters in the play did not cope well, a discussion at the end of the day (the Review phase) enabled the students to explain ways in which to cope, had they been in the same situation. Examples of some of the secrets included:

- A Year 7 student depressed because he has just found out he is adopted
- A head of year who hates children
- A school laboratory technician creating a secret toxin
- A headteacher who was a werewolf.

This SoW ultimately helps to promote empathy, by exploring the emotions of others through the process of unearthing and unlocking what can make people behave in certain ways from the perspective of the characters.

Lesson plan and resources for PSHE SoW

Resources

- 'Make 'n' Mend' from *Stolen Secrets* (see Core SoW resources lesson 1)
- Three or four large school room 'doors' from different areas in school – classroom, prep room, toilets, office door. These could be literal doors if you have an accommodating Design Technology department, or signs representing doors
- Sticky notes
- A box labelled 'Secrets Box'
- Character History Sheets (see Core SoW resources lesson 4)
- GCSE or AS/A2 drama students as actors (if possible)
- Materials for writing

Play in a Day PHSE
OVERVIEW OF DAY

1 Prepare for and Connect the Learning

Overview and 'big picture' for learning. Connect with performances of plays students may have seen in or outside of school. What do we know about plays and playwriting?

Explore different emotions through idea of secrets. Read 'Make 'n' Mend' from Stolen Secrets (see Core SoW resources). Exploration of what the secrets are, what the emotions are and discussion of strategies of how to cope with them.

2 Agree Learning Objectives

- **Know** some strategies for coping with different emotions
- **Apply** these strategies to the characters in our play
- **Plan** how to use these strategies at school and at home

3 Present New Information Through the Senses

Secrets – who's behind the door?

Group presented with three or four large school room 'doors' from different areas in school – classroom, prep room, toilets, office door. Group decide who, in broad generic terms, is behind the door. They can come up with a list as long as they like, e.g. science teacher; year 7 student; teaching assistant etc. Record ideas on IWB. Link to broad character terms of 'Mother' and 'Daughter' in 'Make 'n' Mend'. Students work in pairs and decide what the different characters' secrets are. Post secrets into the 'Secret Box'. Teacher picks the secrets out of the box, divides them up and hands to groups. The groups have to decide which secret belongs to which character. Students stick secrets up on role on the wall outlines of characters stuck on the walls.

Whole class decide on the most interesting characters, based on their secrets. Shortlist of four or five agreed and main character identified.

4 Construct

In this part of the day the focus is first on generating character histories for our shortlist of characters. Students work in small groups on this. Each group should be allocated a character to generate their character history (see Core SoW resources for character history sheets).

Then revisit the characters' secrets. How would the characters cope with the secrets they have? What emotions would be generated? What strategies could they employ for coping with these emotions? Would that character be able to cope?

Workshop session with GCSE/AS/A2 drama students as actors, exploring how characters respond in two different scenes. Focus on their secrets. How do their secrets affect how they behave in these different scenarios?

The TEEP Learning Cycle

5 Apply to Demonstrate your New Understanding

First scene, exploring secrets and emotions, written as a whole group based on improvised workshop session earlier. Focus on secrets as dramatic devices and how they propel the action forward. Also explore how entrances and exits of characters can do this. At the end of the scene, something must have changed for the protagonist.

Group decide what the next four things are that will happen, and what the story will be. Group map out story of play, including locations in school (using the doors if you like), characters, and how the secret of the main character will be revealed and explored as the play progresses.

Group split into four, relating to one of the four things/events that happen (this depends on the size of your group), and write a scene each. Each group is supported by a member of staff.

Come back together. Read play so far. Final scene written as a whole group again.

6 Review – step back and reflect on your learning

Actors return to read through play.

Performance of play to an audience.

Reflection of skills and coping strategies learnt.

Day ends.

Play in a Day PSHE SoW

Please use this detailed plan alongside the overview of the day.

1 Prepare for Learning and 2 Agree Learning Objectives – approx 45 minutes in all. Allow enough time to read the scene – it will provoke a lot of discussion and ideas.

Learning Objectives:

* Know some strategies for coping with different emotions
* Apply these strategies to the characters in our play
* Plan how to use these strategies at school and at home.

Students and teachers sitting in a circle.

Teacher gives the big picture and overview for learning, including learning objectives. Explain how we will be exploring different emotions and feelings today *through* writing a play, so we'll learn all about the craft of playwriting too. Use this as an opportunity to tie into any further themes that you may have been exploring in PSHE or assemblies in school. The idea of coping with emotions and strategies for coping with emotions must be revisited throughout the day.

Question the group about what they know about plays and playwriting, and connect with any performances they may have seen in or outside school. Record ideas on IWB or flipchart. Focus on dramatic structure, characters, location and also what plays look like on the page. How do we know a text is a play? What does it look like? What does a play have? Where are plays performed? (e.g. they don't have to be performed in a theatre!) Keep fast pace here.

Teacher explains that today we're going to explore the idea of emotions and secrets. To get us started, we're going to play Chinese Whispers. Teacher starts off silly 'secret'. 'Secret' passed around. What was it? Are secrets always silly? How can secrets make us feel?

We're now going to explore a secret in a short extract from a play written by a playwright working with year 10 students in a school in London.

We're going to think about how the secret in the extract affects how the characters feel. How do the characters cope with the secret? Read extract with students. What is the daughter really hiding? Why can't she be direct with her mother? Do you think she has a secret? If so, what could it be? How could she cope with this? Reference first learning objective. Can we achieve this learning objective? How? What do we know now? What have we learnt from each other?

3 Present New Information Through All the Senses – approx. 30–40 minutes

Teacher explains that we're now going to think about characters in our *own* play and what secrets they might have. Reference second learning objective. Our play will be set in school, and initially we're going to think about our characters in very broad terms. They haven't got names yet; we don't know anything about them. At the moment, we only know them in broad terms like the names of 'Mother' and 'Daughter' in *Make 'n' Mend*. So it might be 'Year 7 student' or 'Dinner lady' etc.

Present the group with four (or more) different 'doors'. These could be literal (if you have a very willing and helpful Design Technology department!), photographs of doors around school or drawn doors on large sheets of paper pinned up on the walls. Explain that each door represents a door in school. Where are the doors? Who is behind them? Remind pupils we are thinking of characters not real people. Generate a list of six to eight characters behind the doors. Explain that each character has a secret. What do we think the secrets are? Students work in pairs and write the secrets on sticky notes, one secret per sticky note. Don't write the character on the sticky note. Students post secrets in 'Secret Box'. While students are doing this, a teacher or teaching assistant should write the characters, e.g. 'Year 7 pupil', 'History teacher' etc. above large outlines of people pinned up around the room. These "people" will become characters in the play.

Divide up secrets from box and hand to students randomly. They will end up with secrets they haven't written. Around the room are outlines of characters. Students decide which secrets belong to which characters and stick them up on the outlines of characters.

Class decides who the most interesting character is and why. (It will probably be the character with the most secrets!) Who will be our protagonist, our main character? Class votes on main characters and what their big secrets are.

Group decides what the secrets of the other characters are. Write in pen on each character.

4 Construct – approx. 60 minutes

Teacher explains that we know who our characters are, and we know what their secrets are. But we don't know what their names are or anything else about them. Their secrets will probably enable us to find out more about them. Now we're going to explore our characters in further detail. Explain character history sheet. Have these copied onto A3. Split into groups of four. Each group is allocated a character and works through character history sheets.

Feedback. Spokesperson from each group reads out three or four most important things about their character. Another teacher/teaching assistant scribes this on character outlines on wall. Reference second learning objective. Given what we know about our characters now, how would they cope with the secrets they have? What emotions would be generated? What strategies would they use for coping with these emotions? Would they be able to cope? Record the ideas for coping with emotions on the IWB or flipchart.

Explain to group that we now have a clearer idea of our characters and their backgrounds. We are now going to work with our GCSE/AS/A2 actors to help explore our characters in more detail to enable us to write the first scene together.

The actors should improvise two scenes based on the characters the writers have come up with, and the writers need to provide the actors with the following:

1. Each character's secret
2. The location of the scene

3.   The time/setting
4.   Some background information about the characters based on the character histories
5.   Some information about the relationships – do the characters know each other?
6.   An objective for each character – something the character wants/ needs.

The students could then question the actors (who are in role as the characters) and find out how their characters feel. This could be set up as a Jeremy Kyle-type scenario with the students asking the actors in character a question. The 'theme' of the Jeremy Kyle programme could be the secret of one of the characters – e.g. 'In today's show we're dealing with hidden secrets … I Want to Leave School and Join the Circus … and I'm Only 12!!'

5 Apply to Demonstrate Your New Understanding – approx. 90 minutes in all

So now we've got a detailed, clearer picture of our characters and how they respond in different scenarios. We now need to apply all these ideas about our characters and their secrets and emotions to our play. We're going to write the first scene together based on the scenes that were improvised and then split into groups and write a scene each. Our main character will be in the first scene. Explain that something must have changed for the main character by the end of the scene (this is vital).

Take a starting point for the scene from the improvised work that has taken place earlier. Again, get the students to consider:

1.   Each character's secret
2.   The location of the scene
3.   The time/setting
4.   Where have the characters come from?
5.   Some information about the relationships – do the characters know each other?
6.   An objective for each character – something the character wants/ needs.

Once they have decided on the location (e.g. in school, but where in school?), the time of day and the month/season, this can be written at the top of the scene as a stage direction, e.g.:

> *A crowded school canteen on a cold winter's day. Students are rushing to get something to eat and there is a lot of noise, along with wet feet and umbrellas. Some students are very wet from the heavy rain.*

Encourage the students to think about how the characters would react in the different situations that have started to emerge. Teacher or student scribes on the board/IWB the scene that begins to emerge. Characters react to each other, and it is understanding that theatre is about action in the present, and what the characters are deciding to do in that moment, that is being explored here.

It is very useful to focus on entrances and exits of characters. Use an entrance of a character to introduce conflict and something new to the scene, related to the characters' secrets, e.g.:

Teacher: You're late.

Pupil (out of breath): Sorry, sir.

Teacher: Sorry isn't good enough. Why are you so late?

Pupil: Why are you so interested? (Looks down at bulging bag). I can't tell you. I'm here now anyway, so what's the problem?

Ask the students to read out the scene. How are the characters' secrets being used as dramatic devices? How are they propelling the action forward? How are the secrets creating conflict? These are vital questions for the students to consider in generating drama. Add or remove any lines in response to these questions.

Scene ends.

This strategy demonstrates how subtext is revealed through action rather than exposition as well as getting students to think about location as a character and another driving force behind the narrative.

In this exercise they have written dialogue, been introduced to character, location, subtext etc. and they have seen how a scene is written.

It's now vital that what happens in the play is mapped out. This must take into account secrets and emotions, and how characters would respond.

There will be six more 'events', and each event will be a scene (this can be less depending on the time you have and the size of your group). Group decides what will happen, what secrets are involved, what each event will be, what characters will be involved, and what emotions are involved in the scene and how the characters cope with those emotions. Map this out or bullet-point it in order on the IWB. Refer to the ideas about coping with emotions from earlier in the day. Teacher records events and information on the board, bullet-pointed. The final scene will be written by everyone together.

Teacher splits class into groups of about four and allocates each group a scene/event. Ensure they think about the secret, the location (they can use the doors from earlier to help if they like) and how the characters would respond in that location and situation. Groups have sugar paper and large felts to write their scene. Groups need enough space to do this.

Each group is supported by a member of staff (where possible).

Come back together as a group. Read play so far. Does it make sense? Is there anything missing? Do we need to include anything else? Spend some time back in groups re-writing.

Come back together and write final scene of play as a group. What happens? What resolution is there? Is there any resolution? What has the main character learned, maybe about him/herself?

6 Review

Last lesson of day – read through and workshop performance.

The actors return from earlier and read through all of the scenes.

Performance of play to audience.

Teacher leads reflection time (reference third learning objective) at end of the day with the students to consider what they have learnt during the process of today about coping with emotions, and how they might apply it in everyday life.

Day ends.

7

Moving beyond the KS3 curriculum: connecting with a qualification SoW

Introduction to connecting with a qualification SoW

This SoW starts to look at ways of connecting the plays that are written with possible concrete outcomes in the form of units towards a qualification. We hope that this SoW can begin to pave the way for the Core SoW towards its next phase, that of finding a path into English GCSEs. The SoW has been piloted with students at Batmans Hill Pupil Referral Unit in Tipton, West Midlands and was led by Joshua Dalledonne, Playwriting Officer at Birmingham Repertory Theatre. Batmans Hill Unit provides for young women aged 14–19 years who are pregnant or who have children. Students developed plays that were used for the Creative Writing unit of the 'Step Up' (Skills Towards Enabling Progression) qualification through the Open College Network. The students included their work developed in this SoW in their portfolios towards this qualification, where the outcomes are based on the Adult Literacy Core Curriculum. Thus, this SoW is different to the others in that it has both learning objectives and learning outcomes, all derived from the assessment criteria and learning outcomes of the course and the Adult Literacy Core Curriculum.

The first lesson requires both the teacher and the students to have done some preparation. The teacher needs to bring in examples of fiction and works of non-fiction and we suggest a range of newspapers, novels, plays, travel writing and recipe cards etc. A mixture of local and national newspapers including broadsheets should be used to offer a range of stories the students might have personal connections with, and news items that have a wider national and international impact. When choosing extracts from novels we recommend first-person narratives, which will contrast with the play extracts that often offer multiple character interaction. There is a selection of extracts in the Core SoW resources that can be used, and a range of styles such as *Stolen Secrets* and *Baby Girl*.

Students should be asked in advance to bring with them an object that has significant meaning to them or an article that has grabbed their interest in recent days. Students at Batmans Hill provided a range of material from scans of their babies to articles about a woman who had been in the news recently for putting a neighbour's cat in a wheelie bin. The objective of generating the backstories for the artefacts in the third section of the lesson plan is to get multiple interpretations and ideas about what could have happened and what the history and the stories behind these objects are. All the ideas are valid, and this is about exchanging and sharing ideas in preparation for deciding what the story of their play is. A mixture of stories began to emerge at Batmans Hill, and a fusion of times and ideas for plays:

'Henry VIII's wife gives birth to a cat. He wants to kill the cat but his wife doesn't want the cat dead so she drugs her husband.'

'Barack Obama visits Henry VIII in the sixteenth century and wants to steal one of his wives...'

The first lesson also invites the students to consider their stories in a very visual, kinaesthetic way, through a mood or ideas box. This is essentially a box that crystallises all their thoughts and ideas into one place, where images, symbols, text and artefacts combine to make the essence of their emerging stories. The box is referred to throughout the SoW and should become an evolving document of their ideas and thoughts as their thinking and learning progresses. It helpfully acts as a visual reminder to aid reflection in the Review phase of the lesson in particular.

In preparation for the second lesson the teacher needs to gather items for the box of random objects. These should include everyday items such as train tickets and mobile phones as well as the more unusual such as an oil lamp or a pressed flower. Again, this very visual, kinaesthetic strategy enables students to more easily visualise the emerging story and consider the potential significance and impact of the object as a dramatic device. In addition to introducing how to develop a scene with the students, the fifth phase of the lesson also demonstrates the layout of a script, and reading the extracts reinforces this.

The SoW provides students with more than the three stimuli required (personal memories and things that hold special significance to them, newspapers, the objects in the box, exchanging ideas, what happens next in a scene) that can be used as a basis for their learning of creative writing through playwriting, steadily building and introducing ideas throughout the lessons. Exchange and collaboration is built into this through the building blocks of playwriting. The declaration of love scene in the third lesson continues to provide students with entry into a play if some students are struggling to decide on what to write about. This takes the playwriting ingredient of location and environment as its starting point.

The workshop session brings together the work already completed, enables students to reflect on their own work through the responses of their peers and begins to focus their thoughts on who their plays are aimed at, their audience. The students should refer back to their work in previous lessons around character histories and use this information as a short introduction before their scenes are read out. Basic information is needed to set the scenes, such as how old their characters are, their occupations, nationality and where the scene takes place.

Extracts from plays can also be used to illustrate writing for different audiences; *Tin Soldier* by Noël Greig in the SEN SoW is written for younger children, whilst *Baby Girl* has a teenage audience in mind. Connection with theatre companies and their work can be included here, and we recommend using current brochures and trips to see plays as examples. Many of the larger building-based theatre companies offer a range of productions including youth theatre performances, large main stage productions, early years work for very young children, adaptations of classic and modern texts, site-specific work and writer-performer productions to name but a few.

The same fundamental tools of playwriting can be found here as in all of the SoW, but with a greater focus on audience: who students are actually writing for. We encourage teachers and workshop leaders to consider this in all the SoW, but the consideration of audience has a particular emphasis in this SoW and its link with the Creative Writing unit of the Step Up qualification. With all of this material gathered, students are equipped to continue developing their plays and look at producing a mini festival of new writing.

Examples of students' work

Shannon Mckayle, a student from Batmans Hill, wrote the following extract as a response to the declaration of love exercise in lesson three.

The boy and girl have known each other since they were in high school and decided to catch up from their school days with a movie.

Man and woman on the movie run to each other, hug, kiss and declare their love. Boys II Men 'I'll Make Love To You' is the soundtrack.

A: Nah man.

B: What's the matter?

A: I could never tell someone I love them.

B: Why?

A: Karh it's awkward, don't yah fink?

B: Nah, not if they both feel the same about each other.

A: mmm, if you say so.

B: Why don't you try it and see?

A: Erm okay...er (coughs) I love you.

Pause

B: I love you too.

Pause

A: Yeah but it's not the same though.

B: How?

A: Karh we don't mean it.

B: Well I do.

Pause

A: naaaaa you don't.

B: I really do.

A: Yeah, if you say so.

B: What?

A: Lowe it.

B: Skeen.

She immediately gives us a clear understanding of who these characters are, their relationship and their objectives at the beginning of the scene by selecting an intimate setting for the characters but with an ambiguous activity. Watching the film is interpreted as an act of catching up with old friends but also misinterpreted as a romantic encounter here.

Maria Price started to develop the following piece at Batmans Hill that could also be used as an extract when discussing the audience in the final lesson.

Scene One

DAUGHTER: I never knew my father. I don't even know his name, who he is, what he does, his birthday. Nothing! I'd like to find out who he is one day. I would like to know why he was never around, I know he's out there somewhere. Every time I ask mom she changes the subject so I don't ask anymore. But he must know about me, surely? Or does he even know he has a daughter? All these questions, I must know. He's out there somewhere, I just know it.

Scene Two

MOM: (shouts) Your tea's on the table.

She takes a swig from a vodka bottle

JESS: (quietly) Thanks.

MOM: (swaying) What time did you get in last night?

JESS: It wasn't me who went out last night it was you!

MOM: Don't back chat!

Takes another swig

JESS: You're always out. If you're not you're slouching with a bottle in your mouth.

MOM: Watch your lip. Look I've made your tea, what more do you want?

JESS: It's the first time in about 2 months. I haven't seen you sober in about 6 months now. There are bills stacked in the hall. I've been doing your washing, there are sick stains all over most of your clothes. When was the last time you had a shower?

MOM: (Stands up swaying) I don't need this from you, you ungrateful little cow.

Mom storms off and Jess starts crying.

Lesson plans and resources for connecting with a qualification SoW

Lesson 1 (Page 148)

Resources

- A range of different forms of writing, e.g.:
  ◊ Newspaper article
  ◊ Extract from novel (first person narrative)
  ◊ Couple of extracts from plays – choose from *Stolen Secrets* and/or *Baby Girl* and/or *My Face* (see Core SoW resources lesson 1)
  ◊ Other non-fiction (travel writing/recipe card from supermarket etc.)
- Students should be asked in advance to bring with them an object that has significant meaning to them or an article that has grabbed their interest in recent days
- Sticky notes
- A number of shoe boxes/cardboard boxes (ideally enough for one each per student) which will become mood/ideas boxes
- A range of craft materials and glue
- Sign saying 'Question Wall' and designated space in room where students can post sticky notes with thoughts, questions and queries about their learning

Lesson 2 (Page 149)

Resources

- Sticky notes
- Extracts from *Baby Girl* and *My Face* (see Core SoW resources lesson 1)
- Pre-prepared box/bag of random objects
- Mood/ideas boxes from last lesson

Lesson 3 (Page 150)

Resources

- Character History Sheets (see Core SoW resources lesson 4)
- Mood/ideas boxes from last two lessons

Lesson 4 (Page 151)

Resources

- Large sheets of paper
- Writing materials

Lesson 5 (Page 152)

Resources

- Extracts from *Tin Soldier* by Noël Greig (see SEN SoW resources lesson 1) and *Baby Girl* by Roy Williams (see Core SoW resources lesson 1)
- A range of brochures from a local theatre with examples of straplines from plays (see lesson plan for more details)
- Sticky notes

Lesson 6 (Page 153)

Resources

- Video of a moving train (if you are able to acquire a clip)
- Train template (see resources)
- Mood/ideas boxes that students have been developing and adding to

QUALIFICATION PLAYWRITING
SCHEME OF WORK
Lesson 1: Generating Ideas
PLTS: *Creative Thinking; Reflective Learning*

---

1 Prepare for and Connect the Learning

Explain project and give 'big picture' for today – it's about generating stories for our plays.

Ref first learning objective. Distribute a range of different forms of writing to identify the differences between a play and other forms of writing and to discuss what makes a play a play:

1 Newspaper article
2 Extract from novel (first person narrative)
3 Couple of extracts from plays – choose from *Stolen Secrets* and/or *Baby Girl* and/or *My Face* (see Core SoW resources)
4 Other non-fiction (travel writing/recipe card from supermarket etc.)

Elicit from students that dramatic fiction is often multiple viewpoints around a situation that is happening in the present. We're witnessing how the characters deal with the situation in front of us. Students work in groups to identify and categorise how they know which ones are plays. What does a script look like on the page? How do you know? What is the purpose of a play? Can it differ? Are plays written to be read or watched or both? Discuss.

---

2 Agree Learning Objectives

Outcomes/Assessment Criteria for this SoW are mapped onto Unit 3 – Creative Writing of the Step Up qualification (Skills Towards Enabling Progression). This is a credit-based qualification which is part of the Open College Network.

Agree Learning Objectives

- **Identify** differences between scripts and other text types
- **Identify** a possible story for a play and **explain** it to our partner
- **Synthesise** our ideas for our stories

Learning Outcomes/Assessment Criteria

- **Identify** some examples of fiction
- **Identify** some examples of non-fiction
- **List** the key differences

---

3 Present New Information Through the Senses

Group Gallery – students stick up on walls and lay out on tables the different artefacts (objects/photos/cuttings etc.) they have brought in to the session. Group spends some time looking at the artefacts and thinking of the back-stories to the artefacts and when they're thinking about the possible stories think about who is/was/could be involved, where they took place and what happened (link to character, place, event).

If you feel appropriate, depending on the personal nature of the artefacts and how well the members of the group know each other, the students label the artefacts with their ideas on sticky notes.

---

4 Construct

Reference second learning objective. Now the group will have looked at everyone's artefacts and thought of some ideas. Students work in pairs and choose one of the possible stories they have thought of based on looking at the artefacts, or choose their own story from their own artefact. Pairs take it in turns to tell each other their story. The partner has to actively listen, making bullet-pointed notes in their journal/book to help them remember if they need to. Each student tells their partner's idea to the rest of the group including what happened, who is/was involved and where it took place (event, character, place).

The TEEP
Learning
Cycle

---

5 Apply to Demonstrate your New Understanding

Reference final learning objective. Students now have some Think Time to consider the story they would like to tell in their play. What is the event/what happens, who is involved and where does it take place? Each student is given a cardboard box/shoe box. The box will be a mood/ideas box for their story and will crystallise all their thoughts and ideas into one space. It can have ideas written on scraps of paper and stuck to it, photographs or drawings stuck to it, objects inside, pieces cut out, symbolic objects stuck on (e.g. a chain of paper clips to represent a chain/constriction/feeling trapped etc.), extracts from Facebook/social networking sites etc. Students can spend some time designing their box based on the ideas for their story, and listing what other things they may need to collect to add to it. They can begin it in this lesson if you have enough materials.

---

6 Review – step back and reflect on your learning

Further Think Time – students write any questions/thoughts they have about the project or about their stories on sticky notes and paste them to the Question Wall – a designated area where students can post questions and reflections about their learning. Discuss as a class.

2 Agree Learning Objectives

- **Understand** how to use personal experience and memory as a source for creative writing
- **Understand** how to use a range of stimuli as a basis for creative writing
- **Apply** what we know about the openings of scenes to the start of our own play

Learning Outcomes/Assessment

- **Identify** personal events that might be used as a basis for creative writing
- **Write** a short piece based on a personal event/memory

1 Prepare for and Connect the Learning

Remind students of the 'big picture' for learning.

Hand out extracts of *Baby Girl* and *My Face* (see Core SoW resources).

Relate to learning last lesson: what type of texts are these? How do we know? What are the presentational, structural and graphological features of texts? Students annotate with sticky notes.

Feedback.

3 Present New Information Through the Senses

Read extracts and focus on the following questions:

What is the relationship between the characters?

What do the characters want?

Where is the scene set?

Discuss.

Focus on *Baby Girl*. If you were to continue writing this, what would the next scene be?

What happens in the next scene?

Who is in the next scene?

The TEEP Learning Cycle

4 Construct

Reference first learning objective and link what has just been read to our own ideas for our stories. Revisit artefacts and mood/ideas boxes from last lesson. Students write a paragraph in their books about their idea and the event, character and place. What does the character want?

Explain that we're going to think in some more detail about deepening the story for our play. Ask the students to imagine an empty room that could be anywhere in the world. There is nothing in it at all. There is a source of light (natural or artificial) and there is a way into the room. Ask the students: What is the shape of the room? What is it made from? What is the 'feel' of the room (smell, atmosphere etc.)?

Have prepared a box/bag of random objects. Ask one student to pick out an object. This object is going to be central to what happens next. Ask a volunteer for their main character from their ideas. 'Place' this character (Character X) in the room the group has imagined. Ask the volunteer to describe them in a little detail. Do the same with another volunteer and a different character, but this character is *just outside* the room. This is Character Y. Character Y now enters the room. Character X says something. Character Y says something. One of the characters leaves the room, with or without the object. What type of change has just happened?

A short scene is thus created in which, through a simple exchange of dialogue, triggered by an object, there has been some sort of change taking place. This is imperative for effective drama.

6 Review – step back and reflect on your learning

Read scene as a class. Further Reflection/Think Time – so what are our ideas for our plays? We've written an opening scene together – has it given us any further ideas? Add further ideas to mood/ideas box.

5 Apply to Demonstrate your New Understanding

Explain to the group that we're going to focus on the second learning objective now and look at openings of scenes. Ask them to think of their main characters and how they might greet someone, e.g. Alright mate; safe; hiya etc. Ask the group for different ways their characters might want to say, 'I don't want to talk to you', e.g. get lost; jog on; see ya; leave me alone etc.

Ask the group to choose one of their characters and the greeting that character would use. This will be the first line of their play and will be the first line for 'A'. Is it the main character? Write this on the board so that they can see the layout:

E.g. A: Hi

Now ask the group to choose one other character and a line that means 'I don't want to talk to you' that would suit this character. This is 'B'.

E.g. B: Leave me alone.

These will be the first two lines of their play:

E.g. A: Hi
B: Leave me alone.

Ask students for a suggestion for the next line for A:

A: Hi
B: Leave me alone.
A: *new line from students*

Continue this exercise so that students continue the play by writing the next line for B and so on. Encourage the students to think about how the characters would react in the different situations that have started to emerge. Characters react to each other, and it is understanding that theatre is about action in the present, and what the characters are deciding to do in that moment, that is being explored here.

QUALIFICATION PLAYWRITING
SCHEME OF WORK
Lesson 3: Location
PLTS: Creative Thinking;
Reflective Learning

1 Prepare for and Connect the Learning

Ask the students to come up with at least ten different locations as a group and write these on the board. Encourage the students to list different locations with different environments and public and private spaces – e.g.:

- a busy train station
- a bedroom
- a church
- a library
- a shopping centre
- a hospital ward
- a garden shed

2 Agree Learning Objectives

- **Understand** how to use a range of stimuli as a basis for creative writing
- **Explain** how the location and environment affects our characters

Learning Outcomes/Assessment

- **List** at least three stimuli which could be used as a basis for creative writing
- **Write** a short piece about a character/place/event using one of the sources identified

3 Present New Information Through the Senses

Link to first and second learning objectives.

Ask the students to each choose one of these locations and write a scene between two characters where one character is declaring their love for the other.

Discuss how the importance of the location will impact directly on the scene and the decisions and actions the characters take. You may need to provide examples here and how public or private locations will also impact greatly. Read out all of the scenes and comment on the location used and how the characters behaved.

4 Construct

Progress check with our ideas for our plays.

Ensure everyone has a paragraph written about their play.

Link to last learning objective.

Explain that in order to progress further with our plays we need to explore our characters in some more detail.

Students create two character history sheets (see Core SoW resources) for their characters.

Share ideas.

The TEEP
Learning
Cycle

6 Review – step back and reflect on your learning

Read a selection of scenes as a class.
What have we learnt about our characters?
How have we learnt it?
What have we learnt about playwriting?
How have we learnt it?
What do we know now about location?
Discuss.

Add any further ideas to mood/ideas boxes if applicable.

Ensure students have finished their scenes (they could for homework) and also that they bring as many copies as there are characters in the scene for the next lesson as it will be a practical workshop lesson.

5 Apply to Demonstrate your New Understanding

Now we've explored two of our characters in more detail, and we have a good understanding of how location affects characters, we're going to write a scene in our play that we are bursting to write. There must be at least two characters in it.

It doesn't have to be the first scene. You need to know who is in the scene, what has just happened and where the scene is set. It is also useful to know what the characters want in the scene – what are their objectives?

Students work individually on their scenes.

QUALIFICATION PLAYWRITING
SCHEME OF WORK
Lesson 4: Workshop Session
PLTS: Creative Thinking;
Reflective Learning

1 Prepare for and Connect the Learning

The space should be markedly different for the start of this session, as the first half will be a workshop session, so it is important to have a well-defined space for performance area and audience.

Welcome group and explain bigger picture for session.

2 Agree Learning Objectives

- **Understand** the importance of choosing a particular reading audience
- **Understand** the importance of drafting and re-drafting in creative writing
- **Reflect** on and **evaluate** our own work

Learning Outcomes/Assessment

- **Identify** an appropriate audience for a short piece of writing and state why the audience is important
- **Comment** on own work, **identify** areas for improvement in light of feedback and **re-draft** our writing as a result of our own and others' feedback.

3 Present New Information Through the Senses

The students should now cast their scene from within the group and the students, as actors, read out the scenes. The students should give a brief introduction to the scene and the characters before it is read out.

Encourage active listening to the scenes – everyone should say something they like about the scene and ask a question, which the writer must not answer but must write in their notebook. You will probably need to give examples of the questions to ask as you go along, or prompt these so that they can unearth treasures in the texts. For example, 'Why does X character wear red socks?', 'Where has Y character just come from?' Encourage them to think about what has changed for each character at the end of the scene.

4 Construct

Write down the names of the students' plays on large, separate sheets of paper (if the plays are named yet; alternatively just write down the students' names separately on sheets of paper). Prompt the students to consider which play would appeal to which sort of audience. The students should consider which audiences their work could appeal to, for example young children; teenage girls; immigrant young people; young mothers etc. They should explain their thinking based on what they have heard so far in terms of the content and subject matter of the plays etc.

The TEEP Learning Cycle

6 Review – step back and reflect on your learning

Share ideas for further scenes.

Are we clear on the audience for our plays now?

Who are we writing for?

Why?

Discuss as a group.

5 Apply to Demonstrate your New Understanding

With this in mind, students should now make any changes or amendments to their scenes that were read out, based on the questions and comments from the other students.

They should then write the scenario for two more scenes. These should be paragraphs with the following information: who is in it, where is it set, what's the starting point for each character (what do they want in this scene) and how has it changed by the end.

Students work individually on their paragraphs.

QUALIFICATION PLAYWRITING
SCHEME OF WORK
Lesson 5: Audience
PLTS: Creative Thinking;
Reflective Learning

1 Prepare for and Connect the Learning

Connect the learning and recap on the last session – have they all got one scene and two scenarios for further scenes?

Revisit what needs to be in the scenario (who is in it, where is it set, what's the starting point for each character (what do they want in this scene) and how has it changed by the end).

Read a few scenarios out.

2 Agree Learning Objectives

- **Understand** the importance of choosing a particular reading audience
- **Reflect** on and **evaluate** our own work

Learning Outcomes/Assessment

- **Identify** an appropriate audience for a short piece of writing and state why the audience is important

3 Present New Information Through the Senses

Thinking and writing time – allow some writing time for students to write these new scenes based on the scenarios they have written.

4 Construct

Revisit ideas about audience from last session.

Read at least two extracts, *Tin Soldier* by Noël Greig (SEN SoW resources) and *Baby Girl* by Roy Williams (Core SoW resources).

Discuss as a group – what age range are these aimed at? Are they different? How do you know? What language is used? What do the characters want?

Summarise comments on board and students record ideas in books.

In pairs, they should now discuss who their plays are aimed at/what audience they are written for and why. They will have begun to consider this last session.

The TEEP Learning Cycle

6 Review – step back and reflect on your learning

Students share some of the new scenes that have been written.

What can we tell about the audience from these scenes?

5 Apply to Demonstrate your New Understanding

Question students – Is there a difference writing a play for a youth theatre, for a large main stage, for early years or for a site-specific production?

Distribute some brochures from a theatre with examples of straplines of plays. Explain the purpose of a strapline and how it crystallises and summarises the 'essence' and story of the play into one line, e.g. 'A poignant and moving portrayal of life in 1980s Birmingham; a play with a dark heart.'; 'A tender and heart-warming tale of self-discovery – Shazia finds the seeds of friendship growing alongside the tomatoes in her greenhouse.' Students should now imagine their own play was going to be produced and included in a brochure to sell the show. They will write a strapline for their play. Write on sticky notes/paper and share at front of class. Add to mood/ideas boxes.

QUALIFICATION PLAYWRITING
SCHEME OF WORK
Lesson 6: Mapping the rest of the play
PLTS: Creative Thinking;
Reflective Learning

The TEEP
Learning
Cycle

1 **Prepare for and Connect the Learning**

Connect the learning and recap on the last session – we should all have three scenes and a strapline.

Share scrolling straplines on IWB.

2 **Agree Learning Objectives – rollover from last session**

- **Understand** the importance of choosing a particular reading audience
- **Reflect** on and **evaluate** our own work

Learning Outcomes/Assessment

- **Identify** an appropriate audience for a short piece of writing and state why the audience is important

3 **Present New Information Through the Senses**

Share a video of a moving train with a number of carriages.

How is this train like our plays?

What could each carriage represent?

Where is its destination?

Discuss analogy of train being like a play and each carriage representing a scene in the play.

4 **Construct**

Distribute train templates.

Encourage students to think about their plays like a train, each scene being a carriage on the train.

Ask them to map out the whole story on the empty train carriages – they should write a sentence for each scene describing what happens (if it's already written) and a sentence for each scene they think they still need to write. Who's in each carriage (scene) to enable the train to get to its destination?

Check ideas/mood boxes.

5 **Apply to Demonstrate your New Understanding**

At this point, depending on where students are with the writing of their plays and the time you have available, you can do the following:

Either

Give them some writing time to finish their scenes.

Or

Gather the students together to look at what plays are emerging. If they were going to put on a festival of new writing for other students, what plays do they have to sell? Is their festival suitable for all ages or would some plays be better pitched at a younger audience? If time allows, students now plan a festival of new writing over the next few lessons or as part of an enrichment activity. The plays should be performed as part of the festival.

6 **Review – step back and reflect on your learning**

As a group, sketch out a skeletal outline for a festival with a strapline next to each play. They also need to consider an outline for what they need to write to finish their play, if applicable.

As part of the festival of new writing, the students' idea/mood boxes should be displayed as a gallery.

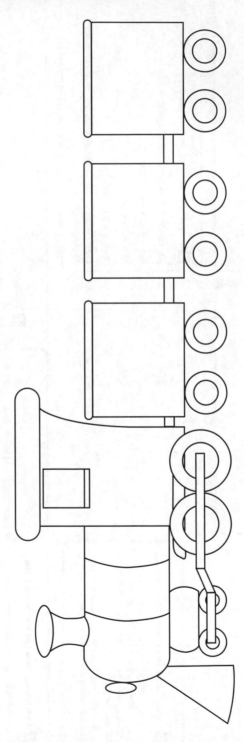

8

Where to next?

This book has offered multiple avenues for introducing playwriting into the curriculum, addressing the needs of different groups of students whilst unlocking individual creativity and personal expression. The SoW enable the tools of playwriting to be adapted to the needs of the students and of the project. We hope this goes some way towards bridging gaps between the educator and the practitioner, and connecting audiences via creative responses to theatre companies. By introducing some newer plays into these SoW, we also hope educators will begin to use more contemporary work within the classroom and subsequently generate new audiences for theatres. Theatre companies that commission new work could begin to see previously under-represented audiences aged 11–14 years eager to see what will be on their stages, and more work for this age group might be produced and subsequently published.

The limitations of one book make it impossible to fully explore the potential for playwriting programmes. Collaborative international playwriting programmes have been piloted between students in Chicago, USA and Birmingham, UK, using an interactive playwriting programme. Theatre companies Pegasus Players, USA, and the Birmingham Repertory Theatre, UK partnered students from Kelly High School, Chicago with students from St Alban's Academy, Birmingham. Videoconferencing enabled joint introductory playwriting workshops to establish a way into exploring ideas, characters and locations for the play before writing this together via a digital playwriting zone. This led to the Birmingham Repertory Theatre being awarded a grant from the Arts Council England's DCD fund (Digital Content Development) to develop a new interactive playwriting zone which offers teachers resources, a blogging section and a playwriting tool and enables multiple writers to write a play together from anywhere in the world. This not only connects international partners but pushes the boundaries of the art form, exploring multi-authored responses to single plays whilst promoting cultural exchange. Connecting students within the same school or different schools and/or community groups is also possible with this, and it is available for individuals, educators and theatre companies to use on a subscription basis (see REPwrite, www. repwrite.com).

We are excited by the potential for playwriting in schools to be an embedded aspect of the curriculum, not merely an add-on. This book primarily explores how playwriting can be integrated into the KS3 curriculum in English and in subjects such as Citizenship and PSHE. We hope that this embedding of good practice, and impact on students' skills particularly in English, will also result in further changes to the English curriculum at KS4. Creative writing is a taught aspect of some of the examination board specifications for GCSE English and GCSE English Language, and traditionally, in terms of fiction writing, many English teachers have focused on teaching students how to write short stories or chapters of novels. We hope that this book will equip teachers with the tools to actively teach playwriting at KS3, and enable them to consider how at GCSE students may also use playwriting to fulfil the requirements of the creative writing aspect of their GCSE English or GCSE English Language course. This does, however, depend on the examination boards recognising playwriting as a medium by which creative writing can be assessed. Interestingly, the guidance for Task 3 of Northern Irish examination board CCEA's (Council for the Curriculum, Examinations and Assessment) GCSE English Language Unit 4: Studying Spoken and Written Language and Writing Creatively states:

Task 3 – Writing Creatively. It allows students to demonstrate the ability to write for purpose using an appropriate format, such as a newspaper article, letter, leaflet, account, diary entry, report, brochure, editorial, polemic, review, commentary, story, *script* or poem.

(*CCEA revised specification for GCSE English Language*, p.10,
our emphasis)

This is assessed by controlled assessment and the examination board therefore set the tasks. It is pleasing that CCEA seem to acknowledge scripts as 'creative writing'; their *Revised GCSE Teacher Guidance English Language Controlled Assessment* (p.12) for Task 3 (Writing Creatively) of Unit 4: Studying Spoken and Written Language states:

Candidates will submit **one** piece for this task. It will allow candidates to write creatively and demonstrate the ability to write for purpose using an appropriate format. We will give the topic for their writing and will change this each year. *The format will be chosen by the candidate depending on the focus of their writing.* The final piece submitted for assessment can take the form of a: newspaper article; letter; leaflet; account; diary entry; report; leaflet; brochure; editorial; polemic; review, commentary; story; *script* or poem. Literary texts can be used as the stimulus for this task.

(*Revised GCSE Teacher Guidance English Language Controlled Assessment,* p.12, our emphasis)

Hearteningly, there is some movement at GCSE level towards the recognition and use of new drama texts since the new GCSE specification changes to English, English Language and English Literature in 2010. One examination board, the Assessment and Qualifications Alliance (AQA), offers Kelly's *Deoxyribonucleic Acid (DNA)* and Samuels's *Kindertransport* as two of its 'modern drama texts' for GCSE English Literature. These are offered as choices alongside more traditional, canonical texts such as *An Inspector Calls* and *The Crucible*.

Another examination board, the Welsh Joint Education Committee (WJEC), offers Whittington's *Be My Baby* and Bennett's *The History Boys* as two of its GCSE English Literature 'contemporary drama' text options, alongside

My Mother Said I Never Should, *Blood Brothers* and *A View from the Bridge*.

The Oxford, Cambridge and Royal Society of Arts (OCR) examination board offers six plays as options for study on its 'Modern Drama' unit of the GCSE in English Literature, Bennett's *The History Boys* being the most modern, alongside stalwarts *Hobson's Choice*, *A View from the Bridge*, *Educating Rita*, *An Inspector Calls* and *Journey's End*.

Northern Ireland's examination board, the Council for the Curriculum, Examinations and Assessment (CCEA), also provides a prescriptive list of plays to choose from to study for Unit 2: The Study of Drama and Poetry as part of the GCSE in English Literature. These are three Shakespeare plays (*Romeo and Juliet*; *The Merchant of Venice*; *Macbeth*); *Blood Brothers*, *An Inspector Calls*, *All My Sons*, *Juno and the Paycock* and the most modern being Friel's 1990 play *Dancing at Lughnasa*.

Edexcel examination board initially appears to be the most radical in offering, as part of Unit 3: Shakespeare and Contemporary Drama of the GCSE in English Literature, a controlled assessment on Shakespeare and a controlled assessment 'Contemporary drama task *on play of own choice*' (our emphasis – *Edexcel GCSE in English Literature Accredited Specification* for 2010 onwards, p. iv). On closer inspection Edexcel does become rather more hesitant, providing 'Suitable examples of contemporary dramas' (ibid., p. 13), none of which are written after the early 1980s. They are: *Whose Life is it Anyway?* (Clark); *A View from the Bridge* (Miller); *Blue Remembered Hills* (Potter); *An Inspector Calls* (Priestly); *Educating Rita* (Russell); *Pygmalion* (Shaw); *Journey's End* (Sheriff). These are, however, only examples, and Edexcel does state that: 'Centres wishing to select their own texts should ensure that they choose a complete and substantial contemporary text. The choice of play must be one that has been professionally published and produced' (ibid., p. 13).

There is also, perhaps, further scope for the incorporation of playwriting within GCSE English Language, not only as part of a 'creative writing' unit. The changes to the examination board specifications have meant that an aspect of GCSEs in English Language is a new focus on spoken language. This involves the exploration and analysis of spoken English in terms of students reflecting critically on language use, language variation and change, regional and cultural diversity and audience and purpose etc. Some examination boards also include *writing* for the spoken voice as well as analysis of the spoken voice (e.g. Edexcel's Unit 3: Spoken Language as part of the GCSE in English Language). Edexcel state that part of the controlled assessment of this Unit will be: 'One writing task: from a choice of speeches, stories with a focus on dialogue, and *scripts*' (our emphasis – ibid., p. iv).

Edexcel itself provides the tasks for assessment. As the specifications are so new, we do not yet know if the board will move towards providing writing tasks for students that enable a focus on playwriting.

The GCSE ball is rolling. It is gathering momentum. We do hope that this book will go some way to introducing English teachers and examination boards to the wealth of exciting plays that are available to study, and also to introducing new ways to both analyse and write plays at KS3 in preparation for GCSE. We hope that this may influence examination boards into reconsidering the plays they choose for study for GCSE English Literature and the tasks that they set for both creative writing and spoken language study as part of GCSE English and GCSE English Language. The SoW and ideas in this book could provide the foundation for this.

The power of playwriting aids personal, social and creative expression in addition to helping literacy. Playwriting has the flexibility to span many areas of the curriculum and introduce students to theatre through their own creative responses, thus creating a new generation of theatregoers. Theatre companies and commissioners of new writing could work in partnership with this new audience and produce more work that challenges and pushes the boundaries of theatre as a living art form. It is this partnership between educators, practitioners and audiences that we believe will successfully embed playwriting into the curriculum.

Glossary

A2 – Advanced Level

AFs – Assessment Focuses

APP – Assessing Pupil Progress

AQA examination board – Assessment and Qualifications Alliance

AS – Advanced Subsidiary Level

CCEA examination board – Council for the Curriculum, Examinations and Assessment

DCD – Digital Content Development

EAL – English as an Additional Language

GCSE – General Certificate of Secondary Education

ICT – Information Communications Technology

IWB – Interactive White Board

KS3 – Key Stage 3

KS4 – Key Stage 4

KS5 – Key Stage 5

NC levels – National Curriculum levels

OCR examination board – Oxford, Cambridge and Royal Society of Arts

OFSTED – Office for Standards in Education

P levels/P scales – assessment criteria to help assess students with special educational needs (SEN) who are working below level 1 of the National Curriculum

PGCE – Postgraduate Certificate in Education

PLTS – Personal Learning and Thinking Skills

PPT – PowerPoint presentation
PSHE – Personal, Social and Health Education
RAF – Reading Assessment Focus
RE – Religious Education
S&L AF – Speaking and Listening Assessment Focus
SEN – Special Educational Needs
SoW – Scheme of Work
SSAT – Specialist Schools and Academies Trust
STEM – science; technology; engineering; mathematics
TA – Teaching Assistant
TEEP – Teacher Effectiveness Enhancement Programme
WAF – Writing Assessment Focus
WJEC examination board – Welsh Joint Education Committee

Bibliography

AQA (2010a) *GCSE Specification English*, AQA.

AQA (2010b) *GCSE Specification English Language*, AQA.

AQA (2010c) *GCSE Specification English Literature*, AQA.

Bennett, Stuart (ed.) (2005) *Theatre for Children and Young People*, Twickenham: Aurora Metro Publications Limited.

CCEA (2010a) *CCEA revised specification for GCSE English*, CCEA.

CCEA (2010b) *CCEA revised specification for GCSE English Language*, CCEA.

CCEA (2010c) *CCEA revised specification for GCSE English Literature*, CCEA.

CCEA (2010d) *Revised GCSE Teacher Guidance English Language Controlled Assessment*, CCEA.

Davis, Rib (1998) *Writing Dialogue for Scripts*, London: A & C Black Limited.

Edexcel (2009a) *Edexcel GCSE in English Accredited Specification*, Edexcel Limited.

Edexcel (2009b) *Edexcel GCSE in English Language Accredited Specification*, Edexcel Limited.

Edexcel (2009c) *Edexcel GCSE in English Literature Accredited Specification*, Edexcel Limited.

Edgar, David (2009) *How Plays Work*, London: Nick Hern Books Limited.

Gooch, Steve (1995) *Writing a Play*, London: A & C Black Limited.

Greig, Noël (2005) *Playwriting: A Practical Guide*, Oxon: Routledge.

Greig, Noël (2008) *Young People, New Theatre: A Practical Guide to an Intercultural Process*, Oxon: Routledge.

Harman, Paul (ed.) (2009) *A Guide to UK Theatre for Young Audiences*, Twickenham: Aurora Metro Publications Limited.

OCR (2009a) *OCR GCSE in English Specification*, OCR.

OCR (2009b) *OCR GCSE in English Language Specification*, OCR.

OCR (2009c) *OCR GCSE in English Literature Specification*, OCR.

Sumsion, Joe (ed.) (2006) *The Skeleton Key*, Cheshire: Action Transport Theatre Company.

Waters, Steve (2010) *The Secret Life of Plays*, London: Nick Hern Books Limited.

WJEC (2010a) *WJEC GCSE in English*, WJEC.

WJEC (2010b) *WJEC GCSE in English Language*, WJEC.

WJEC (2010c) *WJEC GCSE in English Literature*, WJEC.

Woolland, Brian (2008) *Pupils as Playwrights*, Stoke on Trent: Trentham Books Limited.

Websites

APP in English with level descriptors –
  http://nationalstrategies.standards.dcsf.gov.uk/node/16051
AQA examination board – www.aqa.org.uk
Birmingham Repertory Theatre – www.birmingham-rep.co.uk
CCEA examination board – www.rewardinglearning.org.uk
Edexcel examination board – www.edexcel.com
Half Moon Theatre – www.halfmoon.org.uk
National Curriculum – http://curriculum.qcda.gov.uk/
National Theatre New Connections Programme –
  www.nationaltheatre.org.uk/newconnections
OCR examination board – www.ocr.org.uk
P scales – http://nationalstrategies.standards.dcsf.gov.uk/node/169991
Personal, Learning and Thinking Skills –
  http://curriculum.qcda.gov.uk/key-stages-3-and-4/skills/plts/index.aspx
REPwrite – www.repwrite.com
Step Up – www.nocn.org.uk/page/20365/step-up
Theatre Centre – www.theatrecentre.org
Unicorn Theatre – www.unicorntheatre.com
WJEC examination board – www.wjec.co.uk

Reading list

1. Edgar, David (2009) *How Plays Work*, London: Nick Hern Books Limited.
2. Evans, Lisa (2010) *The Day the Waters Came*, London: Oberon Books Ltd.
3. Greig, Noël (2005) *Playwriting: A Practical Guide*, Oxon: Routledge.
4. Kennedy, Fin (2010) *The Urban Girl's Guide to Camping and other plays*, London: Nick Hern Books Limited.
5. Maxwell, Douglas (2008) *The Mother Ship*, London: Oberon Books Ltd.
6. Miller, Carl (2011) *Ostrich Boys*, adapted from the novel by Keith Gray, London: Methuen.
7. Pollock, Alan (2008) *One Night in November*, London: Josef Weinberger Ltd.
8. Various authors (2003) *Theatre Centre: Plays for Young People – Celebrating 50 Years of Theatre Centre*, Twickenham: Aurora Metro Publications Ltd.
9. Various authors (2006) *Shell Connections 2006: New Plays for Young People*, London: Faber and Faber Ltd.
10. Various authors (2007) *NT Connections 2007: New Plays for Young People*, London: Faber and Faber Ltd.
11. Various authors (2008) *New Connections 2008: Plays for Young People*, London: Faber and Faber Ltd.
12. Various authors (2009a) *Class Acts: New Plays for Children to Act*, London: Oberon.
13. Various authors (2009b) *New Connections 2009: Plays for Young People*, London: Faber and Faber Ltd.
14. Waters, Steve (2010) *The Secret Life of Plays*, London: Nick Hern Books Limited.
15. Way, Charles (2005) *Plays for Young People*, Twickenham: Aurora Metro Publications Ltd.